The Kindred of the Wild

THE KINDRED OF THE WILD

A Book of Animal Life

BY

CHARLES G. D. ROBERTS

AUTHOR OF "THE HEART OF THE ANCIENT WOOD," "THE
FORGE IN THE FOREST," "A SISTER TO
EVANGELINE," "POEMS," ETC.

WITH MANY ILLUSTRATIONS BY
CHARLES LIVINGSTON BULL

NEW YORK
STITT PUBLISHING COMPANY
1905

Copyright, 1900, 1901, 1902, *by*
THE OUTING PUBLISHING COMPANY

Copyright, 1901, 1902, *by*
FRANK LESLIE PUBLISHING HOUSE

Copyright, 1896, *by*
H. S. STONE & COMPANY

Copyright, 1902, *by*
THE CRITERION PUBLICATION COMPANY

Copyright, 1902, *by*
CHARLES SCRIBNER'S SONS

Copyright, 1902, *by*
L. C. PAGE & COMPANY
(INCORPORATED)
All rights reserved

To My People

Contents of the Book

	PAGE
The Animal Story ([1]).	15
The Moonlight Trails	33
The Lord of the Air	55
Wild Motherhood	93
The Homesickness of Kebonka	117
Savoury Meats	143
The Boy and Hushwing	159
A Treason of Nature	181
The Haunter of the Pine Gloom	199
The Watchers of the Camp-Fire	241
When Twilight Falls on the Stump Lots	273
The King of the Mamozekel	287
In Panoply of Spears	349

([1]) Included by permission of the University Society

vii

A List of the Full=Page Drawings in the Book

	PAGE
The Animal Story	13
"The sniffings of the baffled bear or tiger"	17
"The inscrutable eyes of all the cats"	25
The Moonlight Trails	31
"All the players were motionless, with ears one way"	37
"It was beyond his reach"	49
The Lord of the Air	53
"He saw his wide-winged mate, too, leave the nest"	57
"Holding the fish firmly in the clutch of one great talon"	65
"Helplessly intertangled in the meshes"	79
"They flocked blackly about with vituperative malice"	83
Wild Motherhood	91
"Led his herd off northward"	95

ix

A List of the Full-Page Drawings

	PAGE
"Stood for a moment to sniff the air"	99
"Around its rim circled the wary mother"	105

The Homesickness of Kebonka . . . 115
"He would stand motionless, his compact, glossy head high in air" 125
"Fell with a great splash into the channel of the Tantramar" 133
"The discourager of quests darted stealthily forth" 137

Savoury Meats 141
"Two green eyes, close to the ground" . 153

The Boy and Hushwing 157
"He struck the empty air" 165
"Settled himself, much disconcerted, on the back of an old haircloth sofa" . 171

A Treason of Nature 179
"He gave answer at once to the summons" 187
"Started in mad haste down the shore" *(See page 189)* . . . . *Frontispiece*
"He dug his claws deeper into the bark, and bared his fangs thirstily" . . 191

The Haunter of the Pine Gloom . . 197
"The big beast little imagined himself observed" 203
"A great lynx landed on the log" . . 207
"Presently the lucifee arose and began creeping stealthily closer" . . . 213
"A silent gray thunderbolt fell upon him" 217
"Yawned hugely, and stretched herself like a cat" 223

A List of the Full-Page Drawings   xi

                                                                   PAGE

"Mounted the carcass with an air of lordship" 229

The Watchers of the Camp-Fire . . 239

"His big, spreading paws carried him over its surface as if he had been shod with snow-shoes" 243

"He pushed the ball again, very, very delicately" 249

"Stole noiselessly toward the shining lovely thing" 259

When Twilight Falls on the Stump Lots   271

"She struggled straight toward the den that held her young" 281

The King of the Mamozekel . . . 285

"The calf stood close by, watching with interest" 293

"The mother mallard would float amid her brood" 301

"But they fell short of their intended mark" 309

"Thick piled the snows about the little herd" 319

"Was off through the underbrush in ignominious flight" 335

"It was fear itself that he was wiping out" 343

In Panoply of Spears 347

"The bear eyed him for some moments" . 353

"A weasel glided noiselessly up to the door of the den" 369

The Kindred of the Wild

Introductory

The Animal Story

ALIKE in matter and in method, the animal story, as we have it to-day, may be regarded as a culmination. The animal story, of course, in one form or another, is as old as the beginnings of literature. Perhaps the most engrossing part in the life-drama of primitive man was that played by the beasts which he hunted, and by those which hunted him. They pressed incessantly upon his perceptions. They furnished both material and impulse for his first gropings toward pictorial art. When he acquired the kindred art of telling a story, they supplied his earliest themes; and they suggested the hieroglyphs by means of which, on carved bone or painted rock, he first gave his narrative a form to outlast the spoken breath. We may not unreasonably infer that the first animal story — the remote but authentic ancestor of "Mowgli" and "Lobo" and "Krag" — was a story of some successful hunt, when success meant life to the starving family; or of some desperate escape, when the truth of the narrative was attested, to the hearers squatted trembling about their fire, by the sniffings of the baffled bear or tiger at the rock-barred mouth of the cave. Such first animal stories had at least one merit of prime literary importance. They were convincing. The first critic, however supercilious, would be little likely to cavil at their verisimilitude.

Somewhat later, when men had begun to harass their souls, and their neighbours, with problems of life and conduct, then these same animals, hourly and in every aspect thrust beneath the eyes of their observation, served to point the moral of their tales. The beasts, not being in a position to resent the ignoble office thrust upon them, were compelled to do duty as concrete types of those obvious virtues and vices of which alone the unsophisticated ethical sense was ready to take cognisance. In this way, as soon as composition became a *métier*, was born the fable; and in this way the ingenuity of the

first author enabled him to avoid a perilous unpopularity among those whose weaknesses and defects his art held up to the scorn of all the caves.

These earliest observers of animal life were compelled by the necessities of the case to observe truly, if not deeply. Pitting their wits against those of their four-foot rivals, they had to know their antagonists, and respect them, in order to overcome them. But it was only the most salient characteristics of each species that concerned the practical observer. It was simple to remember that the tiger was cruel, the fox cunning, the wolf rapacious. And so, as advancing civilisation drew an ever widening line between man and the animals, and men became more and more engrossed in the interests of their own kind, the personalities of the wild creatures which they had once known so well became obscured to them, and the creatures themselves came to be regarded, for the purposes of literature, as types or symbols merely, — except in those cases, equally obstructive to exact observation, where they were revered as temporary tenements of the spirits of departed kinsfolk. The characters in that great beast-epic of the middle ages, "Reynard the Fox," though far more elaborately limned than those which play their succinct rôles in the fables of Æsop, are at the same time in their elaboration far more alien to the truths of wild nature. Reynard, Isegrim, Bruin, and Greybeard have little resemblance to the fox, the wolf, the bear, and the badger, as patience, sympathy, and the camera reveal them to us to-day.

The advent of Christianity, strange as it may seem at first glance, did not make for a closer understanding between man and the lower animals. While it was militant, fighting for its life against the forces of paganism, its effort was to set man at odds with the natural world, and fill his eyes with the wonders of the spiritual. Man was the only thing of consequence on earth, and of man, not his body, but his soul. Nature was the ally of the enemy. The way of nature was the way of death. In man alone was the seed of the divine. Of what concern could be the joy or pain of creatures of no soul, to-morrow returning to the dust? To strenuous spirits, their eyes fixed upon the fear of hell for themselves, and the certainty of it for their neighbours, it smacked of sin to take thought of the feelings of such evanescent products of corruption. Hence it came that, in spite of the gentle understanding of such sweet saints as Francis of Assisi, Anthony of Padua, and Colomb of the Bees, the inarticulate kindred for a long time reaped small comfort from the Dispensation of Love.

With the spread of freedom and the broadening out of all intellectual interests which characterise these modern days, the lower kindreds began to regain their old place in the concern of man. The revival of interest in the animals found literary expression (to classify roughly) in two forms, which necessarily overlap each other now and then, viz., the story of adventure and the anecdote of observation. Hunting as a recreation, pursued with zest from pole to tropics by restless seekers after the new, supplied a species of narrative singularly akin to what the first animal stories must have been, — narratives of desperate encounter, strange peril, and hairbreadth escape. Such hunters' stories and travellers' tales are rarely conspicuous for the exactitude of their observation; but that was not the quality at first demanded of them by fireside readers. The attention of the writer was focussed, not upon the peculiarities or the emotions of the beast protagonist in each fierce, brief drama, but upon the thrill of the action, the final triumph of the human actor. The inevitable tendency of these stories of adventure with beasts was to awaken interest in animals, and to excite a desire for exact knowledge of their traits and habits. The interest and the desire evoked the natural historian, the inheritor of the half-forgotten mantle of Pliny. Precise and patient scientists made the animals their care, observing with microscope and measure, comparing bones, assorting families, subdividing subdivisions, till at length all the beasts of significance to man were ticketed neatly, and laid bare, as far as the inmost fibre of their material substance was concerned, to the eye of popular information.

Altogether admirable and necessary as was this development at large, another, of richer or at least more spiritual significance, was going on at home. Folk who loved their animal comrades—their dogs, horses, cats, parrots, elephants — were observing, with the wonder and interest of discoverers, the astonishing fashion in which the mere instincts of these so-called irrational creatures were able to simulate the operations of reason. The results of this observation were written down, till " anecdotes of animals " came to form a not inconsiderable body of literature. The drift of all these data was overwhelmingly toward one conclusion. The mental processes of the animals observed were seen to be far more complex than the observers had supposed. Where instinct was called in to account for the elaborate ingenuity with which a dog would plan and accomplish the outwitting of a rival, or the nice judgment with which an elephant, with no nest-building ancestors behind him to instruct his brain, would choose and adjust the teak-logs which he was set to pile, it began to seem as if that faithful faculty was being overworked. To explain yet other cases, which no accepted theory seemed to fit, coincidence was invoked, till that rare and elusive phenomenon threatened to become as customary as buttercups. But when instinct and coincidence had done all that could be asked of them, there remained a great unaccounted-for body of facts; and men were forced at last to accept the proposition that, within their varying limitations, animals can and do reason. As far, at least, as the mental intelligence is concerned, the gulf dividing the lowest of the human species from the highest of the animals has in these latter days been reduced to a very narrow psychological fissure.

Whether avowedly or not, it is with the psychology of animal life that the representative animal stories of to-day are first of all concerned. Looking deep into the eyes of certain of the four-footed kindred, we have been startled to see therein a something, before unrecognised, that answered to our inner and intellectual, if not spiritual selves. We have suddenly attained a new and clearer vision. We have come face to face with personality, where we were blindly wont to predicate mere instinct and automatism. It is as if one should step carelessly out of one's back door, and marvel to see unrolling before his new-awakened eyes the peaks and seas and misty valleys of an unknown world. Our chief writers of animal stories at the present day may be regarded as explorers of this unknown world, absorbed in charting its topography. They work, indeed, upon a substantial foundation of known facts. They are minutely scrupulous as to their natural history, and assiduous contributors to that science. But above all are they diligent in their search for the motive beneath the action. Their care is to catch the varying, elusive personalities which dwell back of the luminous brain windows of the dog, the horse, the deer, or wrap themselves in reserve behind the inscrutable eyes of all the cats, or sit aloof in the gaze of the hawk and the eagle. The animal story at its highest point of development is a psychological romance constructed on a framework of natural science.

The real psychology of the animals, so far as we are able to grope our way toward it by deduction

"THE INSCRUTABLE EYES OF ALL THE CATS."

and induction combined, is a very different thing from the psychology of certain stories of animals which paved the way for the present vogue. Of these, such books as "Beautiful Joe" and "Black Beauty" are deservedly conspicuous examples. It is no detraction from the merit of these books, which have done great service in awakening a sympathetic understanding of the animals and sharpening our sense of kinship with all that breathe, to say that their psychology is human. Their animal characters think and feel as human beings would think and feel under like conditions. This marks the stage which these works occupy in the development of the animal story.

The next stage must be regarded as, in literature, a climax indeed, but not the climax in this genre. I refer to the "Mowgli" stories of Mr. Kipling. In these tales the animals are frankly humanised. Their individualisation is distinctly human, as are also their mental and emotional processes, and their highly elaborate powers of expression. Their notions are complex; whereas the motives of real animals, so far as we have hitherto been able to judge them, seem to be essentially simple, in the sense that the motive dominant at a given moment quite obliterates, for the time, all secondary motives.

Their reasoning powers and their constructive imagination are far beyond anything which present knowledge justifies us in ascribing to the inarticulate kindreds. To say this is in no way to depreciate such work, but merely to classify it. There are stories being written now which, for interest and artistic value, are not to be mentioned in the same breath with the "Mowgli" tales, but which nevertheless occupy a more advanced stage in the evolution of this genre.

It seems to me fairly safe to say that this evolution is not likely to go beyond the point to which it has been carried to-day. In such a story, for instance, as that of "Krag, the Kootenay Ram," by Mr. Ernest Seton, the interest centres about the personality, individuality, mentality, of an animal, as well as its purely physical characteristics. The field of animal psychology so admirably opened is an inexhaustible world of wonder. Sympathetic exploration may advance its boundaries to a degree of which we hardly dare to dream; but such expansion cannot be called evolution. There would seem to be no further evolution possible, unless based upon a hypothesis that animals have souls. As souls are apt to elude exact observation, to forecast any such development would seem to be at best merely fanciful.

The animal story, as we now have it, is a potent emancipator. It frees us for a little from the world of shop-worn utilities, and from the mean tenement of self of which we do well to grow weary. It helps us to return to nature, without requiring that we at the same time return to barbarism. It leads us back to the old kinship of earth, without asking us to relinquish by way of toll any part of the wisdom of the ages, any fine essential of the " large result of time." The clear and candid life to which it re-initiates us, far behind though it lies in the long upward march of being, holds for us this quality. It has ever the more significance, it has ever the richer gift of refreshment and renewal, the more humane the heart and spiritual the understanding which we bring to the intimacy of it.

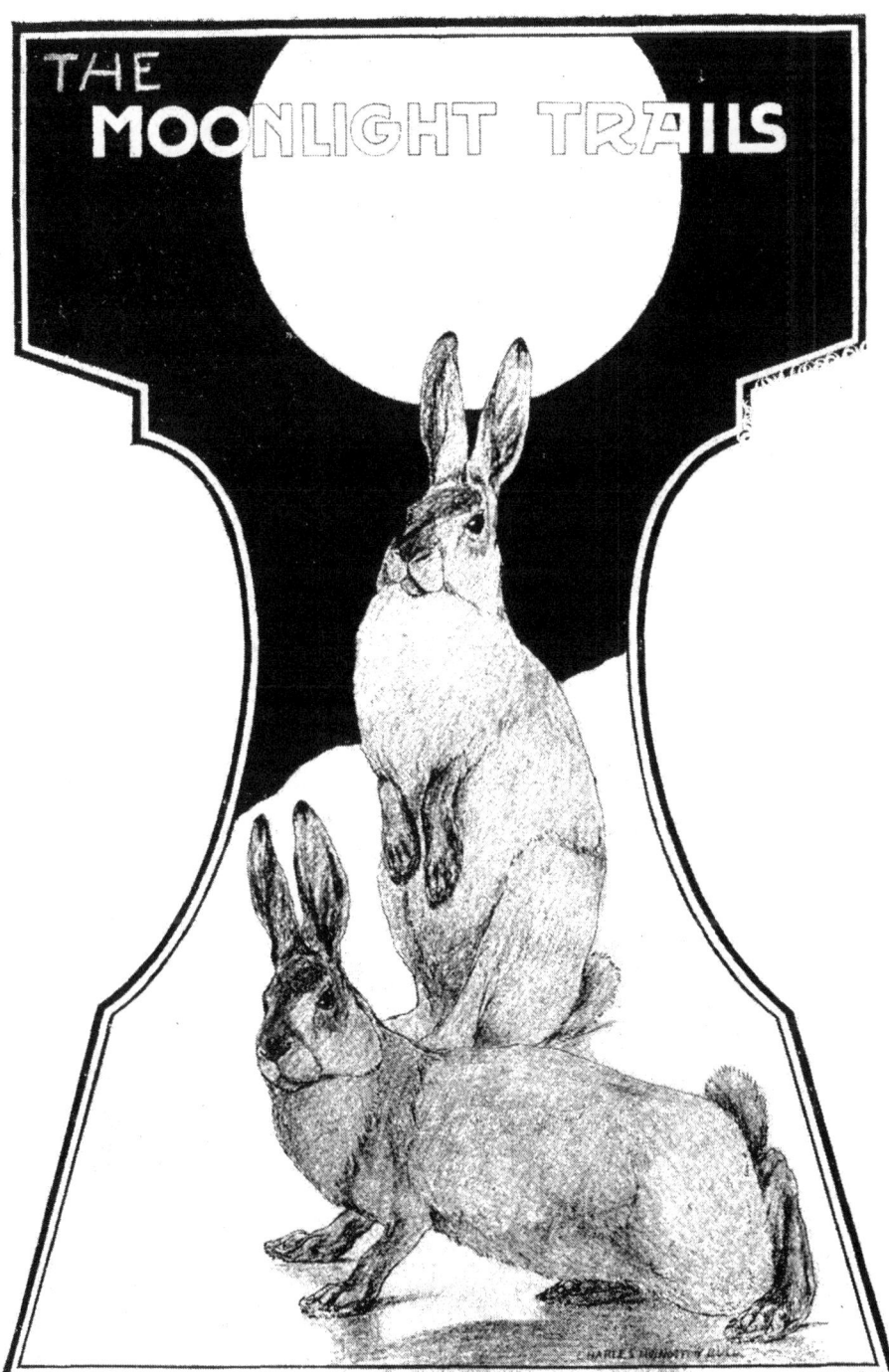

The Moonlight Trails

THERE was no wind. The young fir-trees stood up straight and tall and stiffly pointed from the noiseless white levels of the snow. The blue-white moon of midwinter, sharply glittering like an icicle, hung high in a heaven clear as tempered steel.

The young fir-trees were a second growth, on lands once well cleared, but afterward reclaimed by the forest. They rose in serried phalanxes, with here and there a solitary sentinel of spruce, and here and there a little huddling group of yellow birches. The snow-spaces between formed sparkling alleys, and long, mysterious vistas, expanding frequently into amphitheatres of breathless stillness and flooding radiance. There was no trace of that most ghostly and elusive winter haze which represents the fine breathing of the forest. Rather the air seemed like diamonds held in solution, fluent as by miracle, and not without strange peril to be jarred by sound or motion.

Yet presently the exaggerated tension of the stillness was broken, and no disaster followed. Two small, white, furry shapes came leaping, one behind the other, down a corridor of radiance, as lightly as if a wind were lifting and drifting them. It was as if some of the gentler spirits of the winter and the wild had seized the magic hour for an incarnation. Leaping at gay leisure, their little bodies would lengthen out to a span of nearly three feet, then round themselves together so that the soft pads of their hinder paws would touch the snow within a couple of inches of the prints from which their fore paws were even then starting to rise. The trail thus drawn down the white aisle consisted of an orderly succession of close triplicate bunches of footprints, like no other trail of the wild folk. From time to time the two harmonious shapes would halt, sit up on their hindquarters, erect their long, attentive ears, glance about warily with their bulging eyes which, in this position, could see behind as well as in front of their narrow heads, wrinkle those cleft nostrils which were cunning to differentiate every scent upon the sharp air, and then browse hastily but with a cheerful relish at the spicy shoots of the young yellow birch. Feeding, however, was plainly not their chief purpose.

The Moonlight Trails

Always within a few moments they would resume their leaping progress through the white glitter and the hard, black shadows.

Very soon their path led them out into a wide glade, fenced all about with the serried and formal ranks of the young firs. It seemed as if the blue-white moon stared down into this space with a glassiness of brilliance even more deluding and magical than elsewhere. The snow here was crossed by a tangle of the fine triplicate tracks. Doubling upon themselves in all directions and with obvious irresponsibility, they were evidently the trails of play rather than of business or of flight. Their pattern was the pattern of mirth; and some half dozen wild white rabbits were gaily weaving at it when the two newcomers joined them. Long ears twinkling, round eyes softly shining, they leaped lightly hither and thither, pausing every now and then to touch each other with their sensitive noses, or to pound on the snow with their strong hind legs in mock challenge. It seemed to be the play of care-free children, almost a kind of confused dance, a spontaneous expression of the joy of life. Nevertheless, for all the mirth of it, there was never a moment when two or more of the company were not to be seen sitting erect, with watchful ears and eyes, close in the shadow of the young fir-trees. For the night that was so favourable to the wild rabbits was favourable also to the fox, the wildcat, and the weasel. And death stalks joy forever among the kindred of the wild.

From time to time one or another of the leaping players would take himself off through the fir-trees, while others continued to arrive along the moonlight trails. This went on till the moon had swung perhaps an hour's distance on her shining course; then, suddenly it stopped; and just for a fleeting fraction of a breath all the players were motionless, with ears one way. From one or another of the watchers there had come some signal, swift, but to the rabbits instantly clear. No onlooker not of the cleft-nose, long-ear clan could have told in what the signal consisted, or what was its full significance. But whatever it was, in a moment the players were gone, vanishing to the east and west and south, all at once, as if blown off by a mighty breath. Only toward the north side of the open there went not one.

Nevertheless, the moon, peering down with sharp scrutiny into the unshadowed northern fringes of the open, failed to spy out any lurking shape of fox, wildcat, or weasel. Whatever the form in

"ALL THE PLAYERS WERE MOTIONLESS, WITH EARS ONE WAY"

which fate had approached, it chose not to unmask its menace. Thereafter, for an hour or more, the sparkling glade with its woven devices was empty. Then, throughout the rest of the night, an occasional rabbit would go bounding across it hastily, on affairs intent, and paying no heed to its significant hieroglyphs. And once, just before moon-set, came a large red fox and sniffed about the tangled trails with an interest not untinged with scorn.

II.

The young fir wood covered a tract of poor land some miles in width, between the outskirts of the ancient forest and a small settlement known as Far Bazziley. In the best house of Far Bazziley — that of the parish clergyman — there lived a boy whom chance, and the capricious destiny of the wild folk, led to take a sudden lively interest in the moonlight trails. Belonging to a different class from the other children of the settlement, he was kept from the district school and tutored at home, with more or less regularity, by his father. His lesson hours, as a rule, fell when the other boys were busy at their chores — and it was the tradition of Far Bazziley that boys were born to work, not play. Thus it happened that the boy had little of the companionship of his fellows.

Being of too eager and adventurous a spirit to spend much of his leisure in reading, he was thrown upon his own resources, and often found himself hungry for new interests. Animals he loved, and of all cruelty toward them he was fiercely intolerant. Great or small, it hurt him to see them hurt; and he was not slow to resent and resist that kind of discomfort.

On more than one occasion he had thrashed other boys of the settlement for torturing, with boyish playfulness and ingenuity, superfluous kittens which thrifty housewives had confided to them to drown. These rough interferences with custom did him no harm, for the boys were forced to respect his prowess, and they knew well enough that kittens had some kind of claim upon civilisation. But when it came to his overbearing championship of snakes, that was another matter, and he made himself unpopular. It was rank tyranny, and disgustingly unnatural, if they could not crush a snake's back with stones and then lay it out in the sun to die gradually, without the risk of getting a black eye and bloodied nose for it.

It was in vain the boy explained, on the incontrovertible authority of his father, that the brilliant garter-snake, the dainty little green snake, and indeed all the snakes of the neighbourhood without exception, were as harmless as lady-bugs. A snake was a snake; and in the eyes of Far Bazziley to kill one, with such additions of painfulness in the process as could be devised on the moment, was to obey Biblical injunction. The boy, not unnaturally, was thrust more and more into the lonely eminence of his isolation.

But one unfailing resource he had always with him, and that was the hired man. His mother might be, as she usually was, too absorbed in household cares to give adequate heed to his searching interrogations. His father might spend huge blanks of his time in interminable drives to outlying parts of his parish. But the hired man was always at hand. It was not always the same hired man. But whether his name were Bill or Tom, Henry or Mart or Chris, the boy found that he could safely look for some uniformity of characteristics, and that he could depend upon each in turn for some teaching that seemed to him more practical and timely than equations or the conjugation of *nolo, nolle, nolui*.

At this particular time of the frequenting of the moonlight trails, the boy was unusually fortunate in his hired man. The latter was a boyish, enthusiastic fellow, by the name of Andy, who had an interest in the kind of things which the boy held important. One morning as he was helping Andy with the barn work, the man said:

"It's about full moon now, and right handy weather for rabbit-snarin'. What say if we git off to the woods this afternoon, if your father'll let us, an' set some snares fer to-night, afore a new snow comes and spiles the tracks?"

The silent and mysterious winter woods, the shining spaces of the snow marked here and there with strange footprints leading to unknown lairs, the clear glooms, the awe and the sense of unseen presences — these were what came thronging into the boy's mind at Andy's suggestion. All the wonderful possibilities of it! The wild spirit of adventure, the hunting zest of elemental man, stirred in his veins at the idea. Had he seen a rabbit being hurt he would have rushed with indignant pity to the rescue. But the idea of rabbit-snaring, as presented by Andy's exciting words, fired a side of his imagination so remote from pity as to have no communication with it whatever along the nerves of sympathy or association. He was a vigorous and normal boy, and the jewel of consistency (which is usually paste) was therefore of as little consequence to him as to the most enlightened of his elders. He threw himself with fervour into Andy's scheme, plied him with exhaustive questions as to the methods of making and setting snares, and spent the rest of the morning, under direction, in whittling with his pocket-knife the required uprights and cross-pieces, and twisting the deadly nooses of fine copper wire. In the prime of the afternoon the two, on their snowshoes, set off gaily for the wood of the young fir-trees.

Up the long slope of the snowy pasture lots, where the drifted hillocks sparkled crisply, and the black stumps here and there broke through in suggestive, fantastic shapes, and the gray rampikes towered bleakly to the upper air, the two climbed with brisk steps, the dry cold a tonic to nerve and vein. As they entered the fir woods a fine, balsamy tang breathed up to greet them, and the boy's nostrils took eager note of it.

The first tracks to meet their eyes were the delicate footprints of the red squirrel, ending abruptly at the foot of a tree somewhat larger than its fellows. Then the boy's sharp eyes marked a trail very slender and precise — small, clear dots one after the other; and he had a feeling of protective tenderness to the maker of that innocent little trail, till Andy told him that he of the dainty footprints was the bloodthirsty and indomitable weasel, the scourge of all the lesser forest kin.

The weasel's trail led them presently to another track, consisting of those triplicate clusters of prints, dropped lightly and far apart; and Andy said, " Rabbits! and the weasel's after them! " The words made a swift picture in the boy's imagination; and he never forgot the trail of the wild rabbit or the trail of the weasel.

Crossing these tracks, they soon came to one more beaten, along which it was plain that many rabbits had fared. This they followed, one going on either side of it that it might not be obliterated by the broad trail of their snowshoes; and in a little time it led them out upon the sheltered glade whereon the merrymakers of the night before had held their revels.

In the unclouded downpour of the sunlight the tracks stood forth with emphasised distinctness, a melting, vapourous violet against the gold-white of the snowy surface; and to the boy's eyes, though not to the man's, was revealed a formal and intricate pattern in the tangled markings. To Andy it was incomprehensible; but he saw at once that in the ways leading to the open it would be well to plant the snares. The boy, on the other hand, had a

The Moonlight Trails

keener insight, and exclaimed at once, "What fun they must have been having!" But his sympathy was asleep. Nothing, at that moment, could wake it up so far as to make him realise the part he was about to play toward those childlike revellers of the moonlight trails.

Skirting the glade, and stepping carefully over the trails, they proceeded to set their snares at the openings of three of the main alleys; and for a little while the strokes of their hatchets rang out frostily on the still air as they chopped down fragrant armfuls of the young fir branches.

Each of the three snares was set in this fashion: First they stuck the fir branches into the snow to form a thick green fence on both sides of the trail, with a passage only wide enough for one rabbit at a time to pass through. On each side of this passageway they drove securely a slender stake, notched on the inner face. Over the opening they bent down a springy sapling, securing its top, by a strong cord, to a small wooden cross-piece which was caught and held in the notches of the two uprights. From the under side of this cross-piece was suspended the easy-running noose of copper wire, just ample enough for a rabbit's head, with the ears lying back, to enter readily.

By the time the snares were set it was near sundown, and the young fir-trees were casting long, pointed, purple shadows. With the drawing on of evening the boy felt stirrings of a wild, predatory instinct. His skin tingled with a still excitement which he did not understand, and he went with a fierce yet furtive wariness, peering into the shadows as if for prey. As he and Andy emerged from the woods, and strode silently down the desolate slopes of the pasture lots, he could think of nothing but his return on the morrow to see what prizes had fallen to his snares. His tenderness of heart, his enlightened sympathy with the four-footed kindred, much of his civilisation, in fact, had vanished for the moment, burnt out in the flame of an instinct handed down to him from his primeval ancestors.

III.

That night the moon rose over the young fir woods, blue-white and glittering as on the night before. The air was of the same biting stillness and vitreous transparency. The magic of it stirred up the same merry madness in the veins of the wild rabbits, and set them to aimless gambolling instead of their usual cautious browsing in the thickets of yellow birch. One by one and two by two the white shapes came drifting down the shadowed alleys and moonlight trails of the fir wood toward the bright glade which they seemed to have adopted, for the time, as their playground. The lanes and ways were many that gave entrance to the glade; and presently some half dozen rabbits came bounding, from different directions, across the radiant open. But on the instant they stopped and sat straight up on their haunches, ears erect, struck with consternation.

There at the mouth of one of the alleys a white form jerked high into the air. It hung, silently struggling, whirling round and round, and at the same time swaying up and down with the bending of the sapling-top from which it swung. The startled spectators had no comprehension of the sight, no signal-code to express the kind of peril it portended, and how to flee from it. They sat gazing in terror. Then, at the next entrance, there shot up into the brilliant air another like horror; and at the next, in the same breath, another. The three hung kicking in a hideous silence.

The spell was broken. The spectators, trembling under the imminence of a doom which they could not understand, vanished with long bounds by the opposite side of the glade. All was still again under the blue-white, wizard scrutiny of the moon but those three kicking shapes. And these, too, in a few minutes hung motionless as the fir-trees and the snow. As the glassy cold took hold upon them they slowly stiffened.

About an hour later a big red fox came trotting into the glade. The hanging shapes caught his eye at once. He knew all about snares, being an old fox, for years at odds with the settlement of Far Bazziley. Casting a sharp glance about, he trotted over to the nearest snare and sniffed up desirously toward the white rabbit dangling above him. It was beyond his reach, and one unavailing spring convinced him of the fact. The second hung equally remote. But with the third he was more fortunate. The sapling was slender, and drooped its burden closer to the snow. With an easy leap the fox seized the dangling body, dragged it down, gnawed off its head to release the noose, and bore away the spoils in triumph, conscious of having scored against his human rivals in the hunt.

Late in the morning, when the sun was pale in a sky that threatened snowfall, the boy and Andy came, thrilling with anticipation, to see what the snares had captured. At the sight of the first

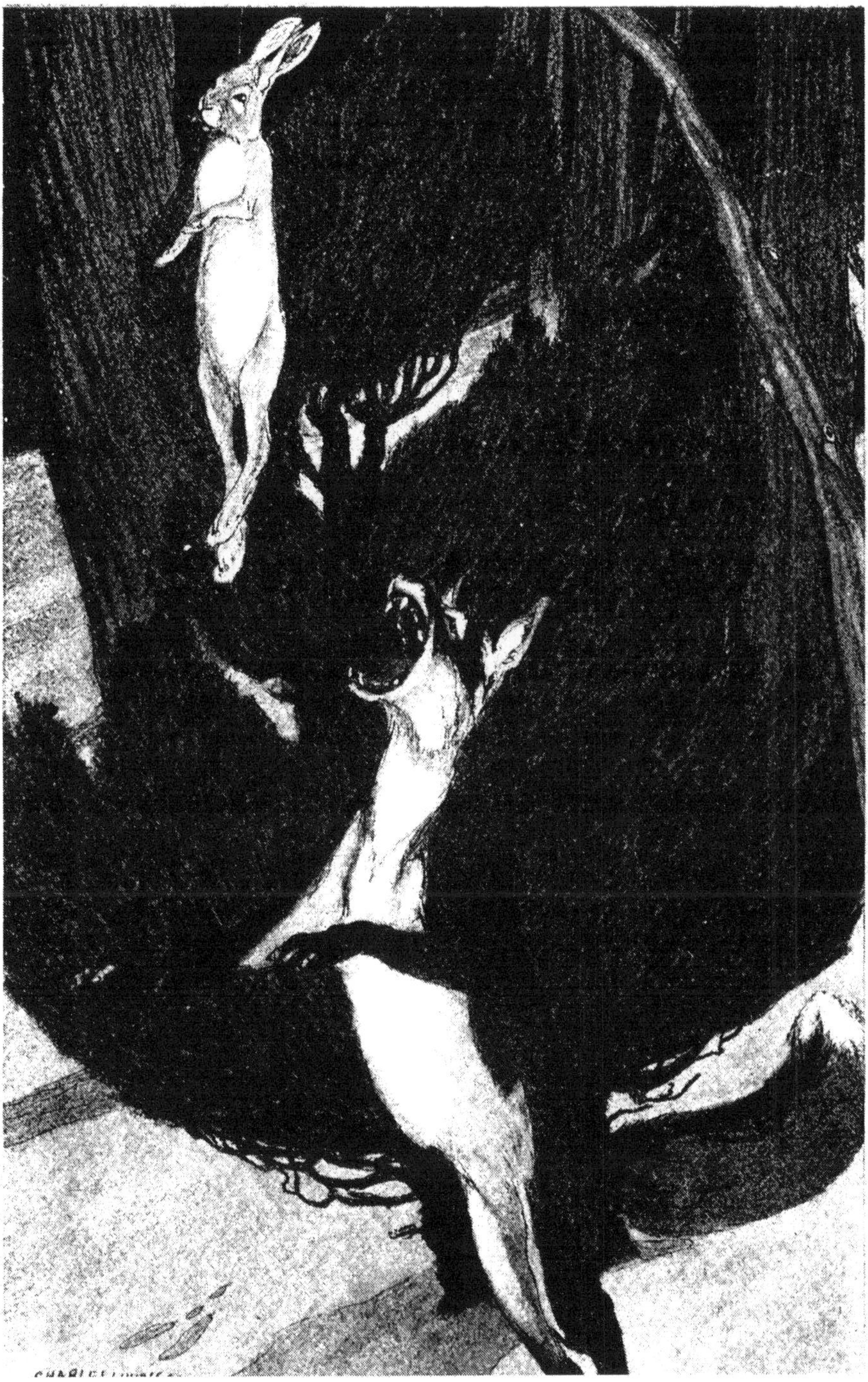

victim, the stiff, furry body hanging in the air from the bowed top of the sapling, the boy's nerves tingled with a novel and fierce sense of triumph. His heart leapt, his eyes flamed, and he sprang forward, with a little cry, as a young beast might in sighting its first quarry. His companion, long used to the hunter's enthusiasm, was less excited. He went to the next snare, removed the victim, reset the catch and noose; while the boy, slinging his trophy over his shoulder with the air of a veteran (as he had seen it done in pictures), hastened on to the third to see why it had failed him. To his untrained eye the trampled snow, the torn head, and the blood spots told the story in part; and as he looked a sense of the tragedy of it began to stir achingly at the roots of his heart. "A fox," remarked Andy, in a matter-of-fact voice, coming up at the moment, with his prize hanging rigidly, by the pathetically babyish hind legs, from the grasp of his mittened fist.

The boy felt a spasm of indignation against the fox. Then, turning his gaze upon Andy's capture, he was struck by the cruel marks of the noose under its jaws and behind its ears. He saw, for the first time, the half-open mouth, the small, jutting tongue, the expression of the dead eyes; and his face changed. He removed his own trophy from his shoulder and stared at it for some moments. Then two big tears rolled over his ruddy cheeks. With an angry exclamation he flung the dead rabbit down on the snow and ran to break up the snares.

"We won't snare any more rabbits, Andy," he cried, averting his face, and starting homeward with a dogged set to his shoulders. Andy, picking up the rejected spoils with a grin that was half bewilderment, half indulgent comprehension, philosophically followed the penitent.

THE
LORD OF THE AIR

The Lord of the Air

THE chill glitter of the northern summer sunrise was washing down over the rounded top of old Sugar Loaf. The sombre and solitary peak, bald save for a ragged veil of blueberry and juniper scrub, seemed to topple over the deep enshadowed valley at its foot. The valley was brimmed with crawling vapours, and around its rim emerged spectrally the jagged crests of the fir wood. On either side of the shrouded valley, to east and west, stretched a chain of similar basins, but more ample, and less deeply wrapped in mist. From these, where the vapours had begun to lift, came radiances of unruffled water.

Where the peak leaned to the valley, the trunk of a giant pine jutted forth slantingly from a roothold a little below the summit. Its top had long ago been shattered by lightning and hurled away into the depths; but from a point some ten or twelve feet below the fracture, one gaunt limb still waved green with persistent, indomitable life. This bleached stub, thrust out over the vast basin, hummed about by the untrammelled winds, was the watch-tower of the great bald eagle who ruled supreme over all the aerial vicinage of the Squatooks.

When the earliest of the morning light fell palely on the crest of Sugar Loaf, the great eagle came to his watch-tower, leaving the nest on the other side of the peak, where the two nestlings had begun to stir hungrily at the first premonition of dawn. Launching majestically from the edge of the nest, he had swooped down into the cold shadow, then, rising into the light by a splendid spiral, with muffled resonance of wing-stroke, he had taken a survey of the empty, glimmering world. It was still quite too dark for hunting, down there on earth; hungry though the nestlings were. He soared, and soared, till presently he saw his wide-winged mate, too, leave the nest, and beat swiftly off toward the Tuladi Lakes, her own special hunting-grounds. Then he dropped quietly to his blanched pine-top on the leaning side of the summit.

Erect and moveless he sat in the growing light, his snowy, flat-crowned head thrust a little forward, consciously lord of the air. His powerful beak, long and scythe-edged, curved over sharply at the

"HE SAW HIS WIDE-WINGED MATE, TOO, LEAVE THE NEST."

end in a rending hook. His eyes, clear, direct, unacquainted with fear, had a certain hardness in their vitreous brilliancy, perhaps by reason of the sharp contrast between the bright gold iris and the unfathomable pupil, and the straight line of the low overhanging brow gave them a savage intensity of penetration. His neck and tail were of the same snowy whiteness as his snake-like head, while the rest of his body was a deep, shadowy brown, close kin to black.

Suddenly, far, far down, winging swiftly in a straight line through the topmost fold of the mist drift, he saw a duck flying from one lake to another. The errand of the duck was probably an unwonted one, of some special urgency, or he would not have flown so high and taken the straight route over the forest; for at this season the duck of inland waters is apt to fly low and follow the watercourse. However that may be, he had forgotten the piercing eyes that kept watch from the peak of old Sugar Loaf.

The eagle lifted and spread the sombre amplitude of his wings, and glided from his perch in a long curve, till he balanced above the unconscious voyager. Then down went his head; his wings shut close, his feathers hardened till he was like a wedge of steel, and down he shot with breathless, appalling speed. But the duck was travelling fast, and the great eagle saw that the mere speed of dropping like a thunderbolt was insufficient for his purpose. Two or three quick, short, fierce thrusts of his pinions, and the speed of his descent was more than doubled. The duck heard an awful hissing in the air above him. But before he could swerve to look up he was struck, whirled away, blotted out of life.

Carried downward with his quarry by the rush of his descent, the eagle spread his pinions and rose sharply just before he reached the nearest tree-tops. High he mounted on still wings with that tremendous impulse. Then, as the impulse failed, his wings began to flap strongly, and he flew off with business-like directness toward the eyrie on the other slope of Sugar Loaf. The head and legs of the duck hung limply from the clutch of his talons.

The nest was a seemingly haphazard collection of sticks, like a hay-cart load of rubbish, deposited on a ledge of the mountainside. In reality, every stick in the structure had been selected with care, and so adeptly fitted that the nest stood unshaken beneath the wildest storms that swept old Sugar Loaf. The ground below the ledge was strewn with the faggots and branches which the careful builders had rejected. The nest had the appearance of being merely laid upon the ledge, but in reality its foundations were firmly locked into a ragged crevice which cleft the ledge at that point.

As the eagle drew near with his prey, he saw his mate winging heavily from the Tuladis, a large fish hanging from her talons. They met at the nest's edge, and two heavy-bodied, soot-coloured, half-fledged nestlings, with wings half spread in eagerness, thrust up hungry, gaping beaks to greet them. The fish, as being the choicer morsel, was first torn to fragments and fed to these greedy beaks; and the duck followed in a few moments, the young ones gulping their meal with grotesque contortions and ecstatic liftings of their wings. Being already much more than half the size of their parents, and growing almost visibly, and expending vast vitality in the production of their first feathers, their appetites were prodigious. Not until these appetites seemed to be, for the moment, stayed, and the eaglets sank back contentedly upon the nest, did the old birds fly off to forage for themselves, leaving a bloody garniture of bones and feathers upon the threshold of their home.

The king — who, though smaller than his mate, was her lord by virtue of superior initiative and more assured, equable daring — returned at once to his watch-tower on the lake side of the summit. It had become his habit to initiate every enterprise from that starting-point. Perching motionless for a few minutes, he surveyed the whole wide landscape of the Squatook Lakes, with the great waters of Lake Temiscouata gleaming to the northwest, and the peak of Bald Mountain, old Sugar Loaf's rival, lifting a defiant front from the shores of Nictau Lake, far to the south.

The last wisp of vapour had vanished, drunk up by the rising sun, and the eagle's eye had clear command of every district of his realm. It was upon the little lake far below him that his interest presently centred itself. There, at no great height above the unruffled waters, he saw a fish-hawk sailing, now tilted to one side or the other on moveless wing, now flapping hurriedly to another course, as if he were scrupulously quartering the whole lake surface.

The king recognised with satisfaction the diligence of this, the most serviceable, though most unwilling, of his subjects. In leisurely fashion he swung off from his perch, and presently was whirling in slow spirals directly over the centre of the lake. Up, up he mounted, till he was a mere speck in the blue, and seemingly oblivious of all that went on below; but, as he wheeled, there in his supreme altitude, his grim white head was stretched ever earthward, and his eyes lost no detail of the fish-hawk's diligence.

All at once, the fish-hawk was seen to poise on steady wing. Then his wings closed, and he shot downward like a javelin. The still waters of the lake were broken with a violent splash, and the fish-hawk's body for a moment almost disappeared. Then, with a struggle and a heavy flapping of wings, the daring fisher arose, grasping in his victorious claws a large "togue" or gray lake trout. He rose till he was well above the tree-tops of the near-by shore, and then headed for his nest in the cedar swamp.

This was the moment for which the eagle had been waiting, up in the blue. Again his vast wings folded themselves. Again his plumage hardened to a wedge of steel. Again he dropped like a plummet. But this time he had no slaughterous intent. He was merely descending out of the heavens to take tribute. Before he reached the hurrying fish-hawk he swerved upward, steadied himself, and flapped a menacing wing in the fish-hawk's face, heading it out again toward the centre of the lake.

Frightened, angry, and obstinate, the big hawk clutched his prize the closer, and made futile efforts to reach the tree-tops. But, fleet though he was, he was no match for the fleetness of his master. The great eagle was over him, under him, around him, all at once, yet never striking him. The king was simply indicating, quite unmistakably, his pleasure, which was that the fish should be delivered up.

Suddenly, however, seeing that the fish-hawk was obstinate, the eagle lost patience. It was time, he concluded, to end the folly. He had no wish to harm the fish-hawk, — a most useful creature, and none too abundant for his kingly needs. In fact, he was always careful not to exact too heavy a tribute from the industrious fisherman, lest the latter should grow discouraged and remove to freer waters. Of the spoils of his fishing the big hawk was always allowed to keep enough to satisfy the requirements of himself and his nestlings. But it was necessary that there should be no foolish misunderstanding on the subject.

The eagle swung away, wheeled sharply with an ominous, harsh rustling of stiffened feathers, and then came at the hawk with a yelp and a sudden tremendous rush. His beak was half open. His

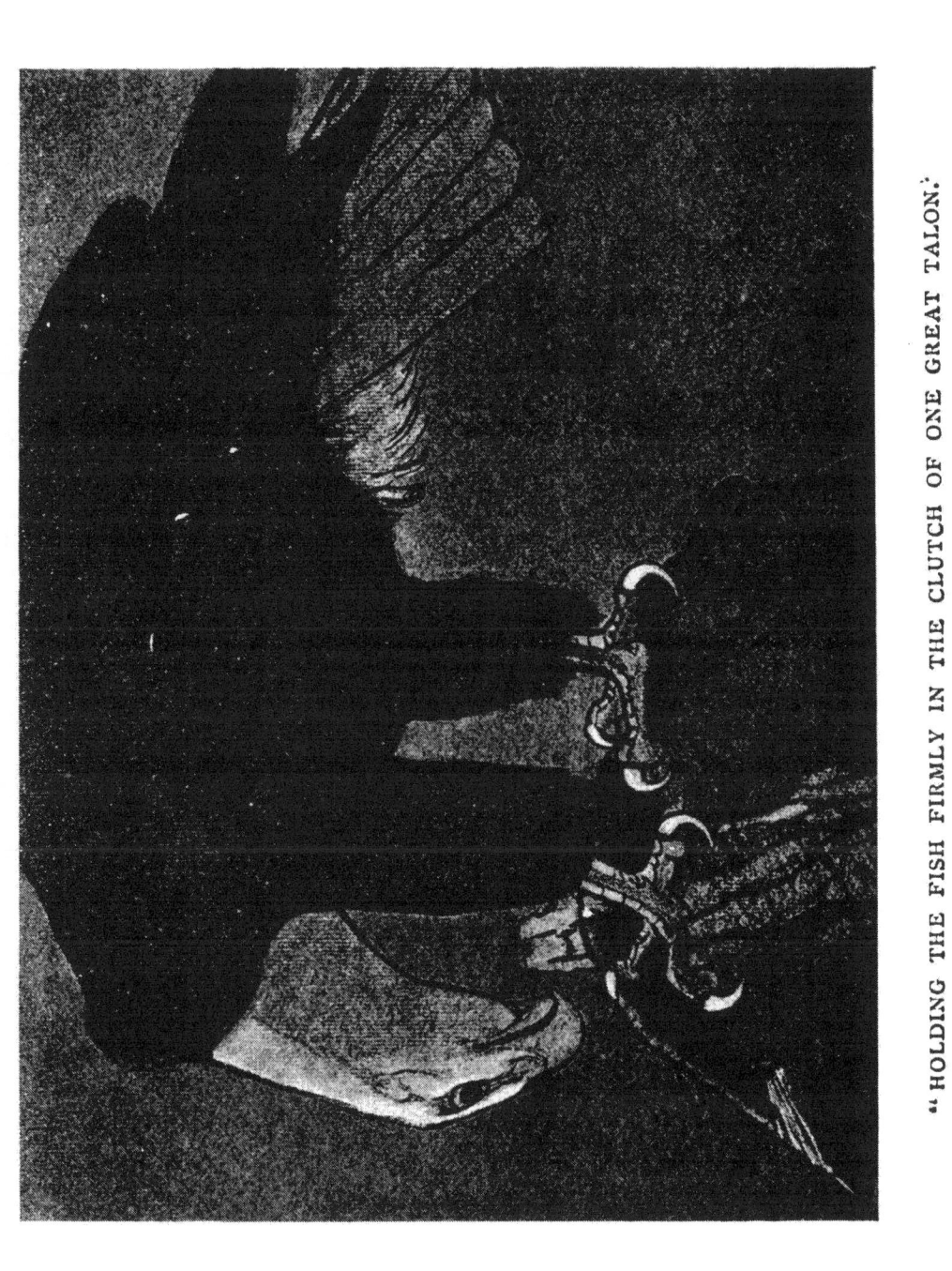

"HOLDING THE FISH FIRMLY IN THE CLUTCH OF ONE GREAT TALON."

great talons were drawn forward and extended for a deadly stroke. His wings darkened broadly over the fugitive. His sound, his shadow, — they were doom itself, annihilation to the frightened hawk.

But that deadly stroke was not delivered. The threat was enough. Shrinking aside with a scream the fish-hawk opened his claws, and the trout fell, a gleaming bar of silver in the morning light. On the instant the eagle half closed his wings, tilted sideways, and swooped. He did not drop, as he had descended upon the voyaging duck, but with a peculiar shortened wing-stroke, he flew straight downward for perhaps a hundred feet. Then, with this tremendous impulse driving him, he shot down like lightning, caught the fish some twenty feet above the water, turned, and rose in a long, magnificent slant, with the tribute borne in his talons. He sailed away majestically to his watch-tower on old Sugar Loaf, to make his meal at leisure, while the ruffled hawk beat away rapidly down the river to try his luck in the lower lake.

Holding the fish firmly in the clutch of one great talon, the eagle tore it to pieces and swallowed it with savage haste. Then he straightened himself, twisted and stretched his neck once or twice, settled back into erect and tranquil dignity, and swept a kingly glance over all his domain, from the far head of Big Squatook, to the alder-crowded outlet of Fourth Lake. He saw unmoved the fish-hawk capture another prize, and fly off with it in triumph to his hidden nest in the swamp. He saw two more ducks winging their way from a sheltered cove to a wide, green reed-bed at the head of the thoroughfare. Being a right kingly monarch, he had no desire to trouble them. Untainted by the lust of killing, he killed only when the need was upon him.

Having preened himself with some care, polished his great beak on the dry wood of the stub, and stretched each wing, deliberately and slowly, the one after the other, with crisp rustling noises, till each strong-shanked plume tingled pleasantly in its socket and fitted with the utmost nicety to its overlapping fellows, he bethought him once more of the appetites of his nestlings. There were no more industrious fish-hawks in sight. Neither hare nor grouse was stirring in the brushy opens. No living creatures were visible save a pair of loons chasing each other off the point of Sugar Loaf Island, and an Indian in his canoe just paddling down to the outlet to spear suckers.

The eagle knew that the loons were no concern

of his. They were never to be caught napping. They could dive quicker than he could swoop and strike. The Indian also he knew, and from long experience had learned to regard him as inoffensive. He had often watched, with feelings as near akin to jealousy as his arrogant heart could entertain, the spearing of suckers and whitefish. And now the sight determined him to go fishing on his own account. He remembered a point of shoals on Big Squatook where large fish were wont to lie basking in the sun, and where sick or disabled fish were frequently washed ashore. Here he might gather some spoil of the shallows, pending the time when he could again take tribute of the fish-hawk. Once more he launched himself from his watch-tower under the peak of Sugar Loaf, and sailed away over the serried green tops of the forest.

II.

Now it chanced that the old Indian, who was the most cunning trapper in all the wilderness of Northern New Brunswick, though he seemed so intent upon his fishing, was in reality watching the great eagle. He had anticipated, and indeed prepared for the regal bird's expedition to those shoals of the Big Squatook; and now, as he marked the direction of his flight, he clucked grimly to himself with satisfaction, and deftly landed a large sucker in the canoe.

That very morning, before the first pallor of dawn had spread over Squatook, the Indian had scattered some fish, trout and suckers, on the shore adjoining the shoal water. The point he chose was where a dense growth of huckleberry and withe-wood ran out to within a few feet of the water's edge, and where the sand of the beach was dotted thickly with tufts of grass. The fish, partly hidden among these tufts of grass, were all distributed over a circular area of a diameter not greater than six or seven feet; and just at the centre of the baited circle the Indian had placed a stone about a foot high, such as any reasonable eagle would like to perch upon when making a hasty meal. He was crafty with all the cunning of the woods, was this old trapper, and he knew that a wise and experienced bird like the king of Sugar Loaf was not to be snared by any ordinary methods. But to snare him he was resolved, though it should take all the rest of the summer to accomplish it; for a rich American, visiting Edmundston on the Madawaska in the spring, had promised him fifty dollars for a fine specimen of the great white headed and white tailed

The Lord of the Air

eagle of the New Brunswick lakes, if delivered at Edmundston alive and unhurt.

When the eagle came to the point of shoals he noticed a slight change. That big stone was something new, and therefore to be suspected. He flew over it without stopping, and alighted on the top of a dead birch-tree near by. A piercing scrutiny convinced him that the presence of the stone at a point where he was accustomed to hop awkwardly on the level sand, was in no way portentous, but rather a provision of destiny for his convenience. He sailed down and alighted upon the stone.

When he saw a dead sucker lying under a grass tuft he considered again. Had the fish lain at the water's edge he would have understood; but up among the grasses, that was a singular situation for a dead fish to get itself into. He now peered suspiciously into the neighbouring bushes, scanned every tuft of grass, and cast a sweeping survey up and down the shores. Everything was as it should be. He hopped down, captured the fish, and was about to fly away with it to his nestlings, when he caught sight of another, and yet another. Further search revealed two more. Plainly the wilderness, in one of those caprices which even his old wisdom had not yet learned to comprehend, was caring very lavishly for the king. He hastily tore and swallowed two of the fish, and then flew away with the biggest of the lot to the nest behind the top of old Sugar Loaf. That same day he came twice again to the point of shoals, till there was not another fish left among the grass tufts. But on the following day, when he came again, with hope rather than expectation in his heart, he found that the supply had been miraculously renewed. His labours thus were greatly lightened. He had more time to sit upon his wind-swept watch-tower under the peak, viewing widely his domain, and leaving the diligent fish-hawks to toil in peace. He fell at once into the custom of perching on the stone at every visit, and then devouring at least one fish before carrying a meal to the nest. His surprise and curiosity as to the source of the supply had died out on the second day. The wild creatures quickly learn to accept a simple obvious good, however extraordinary, as one of those beneficences which the unseen powers bestow without explanation.

By the time the eagle had come to this frame of mind, the old Indian was ready for the next move in his crafty game. He made a strong hoop of plaited withe-wood, about seven feet in diameter.

To this he fastened an ample bag of strong salmon-netting, which he had brought with him from Edmundston for this purpose. To the hoop he fixed securely a stiff birch sapling for a handle, so that the affair when completed was a monster scoop-net, stout and durable in every part. On a moonlight night when he knew that the eagle was safely out of sight, on his eyrie around at the back of Sugar Loaf, the Indian stuck this gigantic scoop into the bow of his canoe, and paddled over to the point of shoals. He had never heard of any one trying to catch an eagle in a net; but, on the other hand, he had never heard of any one wanting an eagle alive, and being willing to emphasise his wants with fifty dollars. The case was plainly one that called for new ideas, and the Indian, who had freed himself from the conservatism of his race, was keenly interested in the plan which he had devised.

The handle of the great scoop-net was about eight feet in length. Its butt the trapper drove slantingly into the sand where the water was an inch or two deep, bracing it securely with stones. He fixed it at an angle so acute that the rim of the net lay almost flat at a height of about four feet above the stone whereon the eagle was wont to perch. Under the uppermost edge of the hoop the trapper fixed a firm prop, making the structure steady and secure. The drooping slack of the net he then caught up and held lightly in place on three or four willow twigs, so that it all lay flat within the rim. This accomplished to his satisfaction, he scattered fish upon the ground as usual, most of them close about the stone and within the area overshadowed by the net, but two or three well outside. Then he paddled noiselessly away across the moon-silvered mirror of the lake, and disappeared into the blackness about the outlet.

On the following morning, the king sat upon his watch-tower while the first light gilded the leaning summit of Sugar Loaf. His gaze swept the vast and shadowy basin of the landscape with its pointed tree-tops dimly emerging above the vapour-drift, and its blank, pallid spaces whereunder the lakes lay veiled in dream. His golden eye flamed fiercely under the straight and fierce white brow; nevertheless, when he saw, far down, two ducks winging their way across the lake, now for a second visible, now vanishing in the mist, he suffered them to go unstricken. The clear light gilded the white feathers of his head and tail, but sank and was absorbed in the cloudy gloom of his wings. For fully half an hour he sat in regal immobility. But when at last the waters of Big Squatook were revealed, stripped and gleaming, he dropped from his perch in a tremendous, leisurely curve, and flew over to the point of shoals.

As he drew near, he was puzzled and annoyed to see the queer structure that had been erected during the night above his rock. It was inexplicable. He at once checked his flight and began whirling in great circles, higher and higher, over the spot, trying in vain to make out what it was. He could see that the dead fish were there as usual. And at length he satisfied himself that no hidden peril lurked in the near-by huckleberry thicket. Then he descended to the nearest tree-top and spent a good half-hour in moveless watching of the net. He little guessed that a dusky figure, equally moveless and far more patient, was watching him in turn from a thicket across the lake.

At the end of this long scrutiny, the eagle decided that a closer investigation was desirable. He flew down and alighted on the level sand well away from the net. There he found a fish which he devoured. Then he found another; and this he carried away to the eyrie. He had not solved the mystery of the strange structure overhanging the rock, but he had proved that it was not actively inimical. It had not interfered with his morning meal, or attempted to hinder him from carrying off his customary spoils. When he returned an hour later to the point of shoals the net looked less strange to him. He even perched on the sloping handle, balancing himself with outspread wings till the swaying ceased. The thing was manifestly harmless. He hopped down, looked with keen interested eyes at the fish beside the rock, hopped in and clutched one out with beak and claw, hopped back again in a great hurry, and flew away with the prize to his watch-tower on Sugar Loaf. This caution he repeated at every visit throughout that day. But when he came again on the morrow, he had grown once more utterly confident. He went under the net without haste or apprehension, and perched unconcernedly on the stone in the midst of his banquet. And the stony face of the old Indian, in his thicket across the lake, flashed for one instant with a furtive grin. He grunted, melted back into the woods, and slipped away to resume his fishing at the outlet.

The next morning, about an hour before dawn, a ghostly birch canoe slipped up to the point of shoals, and came to land about a hundred yards from the net. The Indian stepped out, lifted it from the water, and hid it in the bushes. Then he proceeded to make some important changes in the arrangement of the net.

To the topmost rim of the hoop he tied a strong cord, brought the free end to the ground, led it under a willow root, and carried it some ten paces back into the thicket. Next he removed the supporting prop. Going back into the thicket, he pulled the cord. It ran freely under the willow root, and the net swayed down till it covered the rock, to rebound to its former position the moment he released the cord. Then he restored the prop to its place; but this time, instead of planting its butt firmly in the sand, he balanced it on a small flat stone, so that the least pull would instantaneously dislodge it. To the base of the prop he fixed another cord; and this also he ran under the willow root and carried back into the thicket. To the free end of this second cord he tied a scrap of red flannel, that there might be no mistake at a critical moment. The butt of the handle he loosened, so that if the prop were removed the net would almost fall of its own weight; and on the upper side of the butt, to give steadiness and speed of action, he leaned two heavy stones. Finally, he baited his trap with the usual dead fish, bunching them now under the centre of the net. Then, satisfying himself that all was in working order, he wormed his way into the heart of the thicket. A few leafy branches, cunningly disposed around and above his hiding-place, made his concealment perfect, while his keen black beads of eyes commanded a clear view of the stone beneath the net. The ends of the two cords were between his lean fingers. No waiting fox or hiding grouse could have lain more immovable, could have held his muscles in more patient perfect stillness, than did the wary old trapper through the chill hour of growing dawn.

At last there came a sound that thrilled even such stoic nerves as his. Mighty wings hissed in the air above his head. The next moment he saw the eagle alight upon the level sand beside the net. This time there was no hesitation. The great bird, for all his wisdom, had been lured into accepting the structure as a part of the established order of things. He hopped with undignified alacrity right under the net, clutched a large whitefish, and perched himself on the stone to enjoy his meal.

At that instant he felt, rather than saw, the shadow of a movement in the thicket. Or rather, perhaps, some inward, unaccredited guardian signalled to him of danger. His muscles gathered themselves for that instantaneous spring wherewith

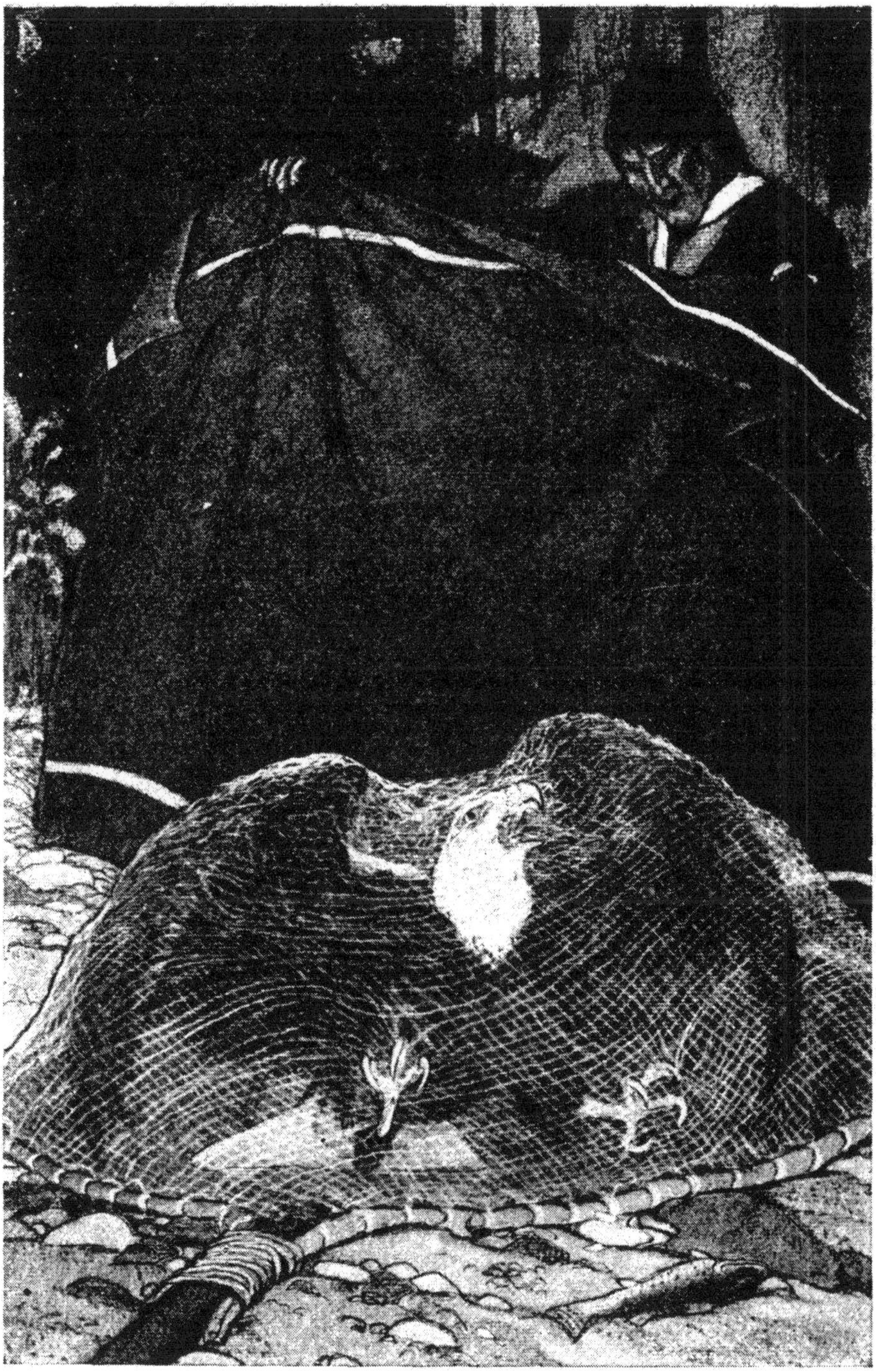

he was wont to hurl himself into the air. But even that electric speed of his was too slow for this demand. Ere he could spring, the great net came down about him with a vicious swish; and in a moment beating wings, tearing beak, and clutching talons were helplessly intertangled in the meshes. Before he could rip himself free, a blanket was thrown over him. He was ignominiously rolled into a bundle, picked up, and carried off under the old Indian's arm.

III.

When the king was gone, it seemed as if a hush had fallen over the country of the Squatooks. When the old pine beneath the toppling peak of Sugar Loaf had stood vacant all the long golden hours of the morning, two crows flew up from the fir-woods to investigate. They hopped up and down on the sacred seat, cawing impertinently and excitedly. Then in a sudden flurry of apprehension they darted away. News of the great eagle's mysterious absence spread quickly among the woodfolk, — not by direct communication, indeed, except in the case of the crows, but subtly and silently, as if by some telepathic code intelligible alike to mink and woodmouse, kingfisher and lucifee.

When the noon had gone by, and the shadow of Sugar Loaf began to creep over the edge of the nest, the old mother eagle grew uneasy at the prolonged absence of her mate. Never before since the nestlings broke the shell had he been so long away. Never before had she been compelled to realise how insatiable were the appetites of her young. She flew around to the pine-tree on the other side of the peak, — and finding it vacant, something told her it had been long unoccupied. Then she flew hither and thither over all the lakes, a fierce loneliness growing in her heart. From the long grasses around the mouth of the thoroughfare between third and fourth lakes a heron arose, flapping wide bluish wings, and she dropped upon it savagely. However her wild heart ached, the nestlings must be fed. With the long limp neck and slender legs of the heron trailing from her talons, she flew away to the eyrie; and she came no more to the Squatooks.

The knowledge of all the woodfolk around the lakes had been flashed in upon her, and she knew some mysterious doom had fallen upon her mate. Thereafter, though the country of the Squatooks was closer at hand and equally well stocked with game, and though the responsibilities of her hunting had been doubled, she kept strictly to her old

"THEY FLOCKED BLACKLY ABOUT WITH VITUPERATIVE MALICE."

hunting-ground of the Tuladis. Everything on the north side of old Sugar Loaf had grown hateful to her; and unmolested within half a mile of the eyrie, the diligent fish-hawks plied their craft, screaming triumphantly over every capture. The male, indeed, growing audacious after the king had been a whole week absent, presumed so far as to adopt the old pine-tree under the peak for his perch, to the loud and disconcerting derision of the crows. They flocked blackly about with vituperative malice, driving him to forsake his seat of usurpation and soar indignantly to heights where they could not follow. But at last the game palled upon their whimsical fancies, and they left him in peace to his aping of the king.

Meanwhile, in the village of Edmundston, in the yard of a house that stood ever enfolded in the sleepless roar of the Falls of Madawaska, the king was eating out his sorrowful and tameless heart. Around one steely-scaled leg, just above the spread of the mighty claws, he wore the ragged ignominy of a bandage of soiled red flannel. This was to prevent the chafing of the clumsy and rusty dog-chain which secured him to his perch in an open shed that looked out upon the river. Across the river, across the cultivated valley with its roofs, and farther across the forest hills than any human eye could see, his eye could see a dim summit, as it were a faint blue cloud on the horizon, his own lost realm of Sugar Loaf. Hour after hour he would sit upon his rude perch, unstirring, unwinking, and gaze upon this faint blue cloud of his desire.

From his jailers he accepted scornfully his daily rations of fish, ignoring the food while any one was by, but tearing it and gorging it savagely when left alone. As week after week dragged on, his hatred of his captors gathered force, but he showed no sign. Fear he was hardly conscious of; or, at least, he had never felt that panic fear which unnerves even kings, except during the one appalling moment when he felt the falling net encumber his wings, and the trapper's smothering blanket shut out the sun from his eyes. Now, when any one of his jailers approached and sought to win his confidence, he would shrink within himself and harden his feathers with wild inward aversion, but his eye of piercing gold would neither dim nor waver, and a clear perception of the limits of his chain would prevent any futile and ignoble struggle to escape. Had he shown more fear, more wildness, his jailers would have more hope of subduing him in some measure; but as it was, being back country men with some knowledge of the wilderness folk, they presently gave him up as tameless and left off troubling him with their attentions. They took good care of him, however, for they were to be well paid for their trouble when the rich American came for his prize.

At last he came; and when he saw the king he was glad. Trophies he had at home in abundance, — the skins of lions which he had shot on the Zambesi, of tigers from Himalayan foot-hills, of grizzlies from Alaskan cañons, and noble heads of moose and caribou from these very highlands of Squatook, whereon the king had been wont to look from his dizzy gyres of flight above old Sugar Loaf. But the great white-headed eagle, who year after year had baffled his woodcraft and eluded his rifle, he had come to love so that he coveted him alive. Now, having been apprised of the capture of so fine and well-known a bird as the king of old Sugar Loaf, he had brought with him an anklet of thick, soft leather for the illustrious captive's leg, and a chain of wrought steel links, slender, delicate, and strong. On the morning after his arrival the new chain was to be fitted.

The great eagle was sitting erect upon his perch, gazing at the faint blue cloud which he alone could see, when two men came to the shed beside the river. One he knew. It was his chief jailer, the man who usually brought fish. The other was a stranger, who carried in his hand a long, glittering thing that jangled and stirred a vague apprehension in his heart. The jailer approached, and with a quick movement wrapped him in a coat, till beak and wings and talons alike were helpless. There was one instinctive, convulsive spasm within the wrapping, and the bundle was still, the great bird being too proud as well as too wise to waste force in a vain struggle.

"Seems pretty tame already," remarked the stranger, in a tone of satisfaction.

"Tame!" exclaimed the countryman. "Them's the kind as don't tame. I've give up trying to tame him. Ef you keep him, an' feed him, an' coax him for ten year, he'll be as wild as the day Gabe snared him up on Big Squatook."

"We'll see," said the stranger, who had confidence in his knowledge of the wild folk.

Seating himself on a broken-backed chair just outside the shadow of the shed, where the light was good, the countryman held the motionless bundle firmly across his knees, and proceeded cautiously to free the fettered leg. He held it in an inflexible grip, respecting those knife-edged claws. Having removed the rusty dog-chain and the ignominious red flannel bandage, he fitted dexterously the soft leather anklet, with its three tiny silver buckles, and its daintily engraved plate, bearing the king's name with the place and date of his capture. Then he reached out his hand for the new steel chain.

The eagle, meanwhile, had been slowly and imperceptibly working his head free; and now, behind the countryman's arm, he looked out from the imprisoning folds of the coat. Fierce, wild, but unaffrighted, his eye caught the glitter of the chain as the stranger held it out. That glitter moved him strangely. On a sudden impulse he opened his mighty beak, and tore savagely at the countryman's leg.

With a yell of pain and surprise the man attempted to jump away from this assault. But as the assailant was on his lap this was obviously impossible. The muscles of his leg stiffened out instinctively, — and the broken-backed chair gave way under the strain. Arms and legs flew wildly in the air as he sprawled backward, — and the coat fell apart, — and the eagle found himself free. The stranger sprang forward to clutch his treasured captive, but received a blinding buffet from the great wings undestined to captivity. The next moment the king bounded upward. The air whistled under his tremendous wing-strokes. Up, up he mounted, leaving the men to gape after him, flushed and foolish. Then he headed his flight for that faint blue cloud beyond the hills.

That afternoon there was a difference in the country of the Squatooks. The nestlings in the eyrie — bigger and blacker and more clamorous they were now than when he went away — found more abundant satisfaction to their growing appetites. Their wide-winged mother, hunting away on Tuladi, hunted with more joyous heart. The fish-hawks on the Squatook waters came no more near the blasted pine; but they fished more diligently, and their hearts were big with indignation over the spoils which they had been forced to deliver up.

The crows far down in the fir-tops were garrulous about the king's return, and the news spread swiftly among the mallards, the muskrats, the hares, and the careful beavers. And the solitude about the toppling peak of old Sugar Loaf seemed to resume some lost sublimity, as the king resumed his throne among the winds.

WILD MOTHERHOOD

Wild Motherhood

THE deep snow in the moose-yard was trodden down to the moss, and darkly soiled with many days of occupancy. The young spruce and birch trees which lined the trodden paths were cropped of all but their toughest and coarsest branches; and the wall of loftier growth which fenced the yard was stripped of its tenderer twigs to the utmost height of the tall bull's neck. The available provender was all but gone, and the herd was in that restlessness which precedes a move to new pastures.

The herd of moose was a small one — three gaunt, rusty-brown, slouching cows, two ungainly calves of a lighter hue, and one huge, high-shouldered bull, whose sweep of palmated antlers bristled like a forest. Compared with the towering bulk of his forequarters, the massive depth of his rough-maned neck, the weight of the formidable antlers, the length and thickness of his clumsy, hooked muzzle with its prehensile upper lip, his lean and frayed hindquarters looked grotesquely diminutive. Surprised by three days of blinding snowfall, the great bull-moose had been forced to establish the yard for his herd in an unfavourable neighbourhood; and now he found himself confronted by the necessity of a long march through snow of such softness and depth as would make swift movement impossible and fetter him in the face of his enemies. In deep snow the moose can neither flee nor fight, at both of which he is adept under fair conditions; and deep snow, as he knew, is the opportunity of the wolf and the hunter. But in this case the herd had no choice. It was simply take the risk or starve.

That same night, when the moon was rising round and white behind the fir-tops, the tall bull breasted and trod down the snowy barriers, and led his herd off northward between the hemlock trunks and the jutting granite boulders. He moved slowly, his immense muzzle stretched straight out before him, the bony array of his antlers laid back level to avoid the hindrance of clinging boughs. Here and there a hollow under the level surface would set him plunging and wallowing for a moment, but in the main his giant strength enabled him to forge his way ahead with a steady majesty

"LED HIS HERD OFF NORTHWARD."

of might. Behind him, in dutiful line, came the three cows; and behind these, again, the calves followed at ease in a clear trail, their muzzles not outstretched like that of the leader, but drooping almost to the snow, their high shoulders working awkwardly at every stride. In utter silence, like dark, monstrous spectres, the line of strange shapes moved on; and down the bewildering, ever-rearranging forest corridors the ominous fingers of long moonlight felt curiously after them. When they had journeyed for some hours the herd came out upon a high and somewhat bare plateau, dotted sparsely with clumps of aspen, stunted yellow birch, and spruce. From this table-land the streaming northwest winds had swept the snow almost clean, carrying it off to fill the neighbouring valleys. The big bull, who knew where he was going and had no will to linger on the way, halted only for a few minutes' browsing, and then started forward on a long, swinging trot. At every stride his loose-hung, wide-cleft, spreading hoofs came sharply together with a flat, clacking noise. The rest of the line swept dutifully into place, and the herd was off.

But not all the herd. One of the calves, tempted a little aside by a thicket of special juiciness and savour, took alarm, and thought he was going to be left behind. He sprang forward, a powerful but clumsy stride, careless of his footing. A treacherous screen of snow-crusted scrub gave way, and he slid sprawling to the bottom of a little narrow gully or crevice, a natural pitfall. His mother, looking solicitously backward, saw him disappear. With a heave of her shoulders, a sweep of her long, hornless head, an anxious flick of her little naked tail, she swung out of the line and trotted swiftly to the rescue.

There was nothing she could do. The crevice was some ten or twelve feet long and five or six in width, with sides almost perpendicular. The calf could just reach its bushy edges with his upstretched muzzle, but he could get no foothold by which to clamber out. On every side he essayed it, falling back with a hoarse bleat from each frightened effort; while the mother, with head down and piteous eyes staring upon him, ran round and round the rim of the trap. At last, when he stopped and stood with palpitating sides and wide nostrils of terror, she, too, halted. Dropping awkwardly upon her knees in the snowy bushes, with loud, blowing breaths, she reached down her head to nose and comfort him with her sensitive muzzle. The calf leaned up as

"STOOD FOR A MOMENT TO SNIFF THE AIR."

close as possible to her caresses. Under their tenderness the tremblings of his gaunt, pathetic knees presently ceased. And in this position the two remained almost motionless for an hour, under the white, unfriendly moon. The herd had gone on without them.

II.

In the wolf's cave in the great blue and white wall of plaster-rock, miles back beside the rushing of the river, there was famine. The she-wolf, heavy and near her time, lay agonising in the darkest corner of the cave, licking in grim silence the raw stump of her right foreleg. Caught in a steel trap, she had gnawed off her own paw as the price of freedom. She could not hunt; and the hunting was bad that winter in the forests by the blue and white wall. The wapiti deer had migrated to safer ranges, and her gray mate, hunting alone, was hard put to it to keep starvation from the cave.

The gray wolf trotted briskly down the broken face of the plaster-rock, in the full glare of the moon, and stood for a moment to sniff the air that came blowing lightly but keenly over the stiff tops of the forest. The wind was clean. It gave him no tidings of a quarry. Descending hurriedly the last fifty yards of the slope, he plunged into the darkness of the fir woods. Soft as was the snow in those quiet recesses, it was yet sufficiently packed to support him as he trotted, noiseless and alert, on the broad-spreading pads of his paws. Furtive and fierce, he slipped through the shadow like a ghost. Across the open glades he fleeted more swiftly, a bright and sinister shape, his head swinging a little from side to side, every sense upon the watch. His direction was pretty steadily to the west of north.

He had travelled long, till the direction of the moon-shadows had taken a different angle to his path, when suddenly there came a scent upon the wind. He stopped, one foot up, arrested in his stride. The gray, cloudy brush of his tail stiffened out. His nostrils, held high to catch every waft of the new scent, dilated; and the edges of his upper lip came down over the white fangs, from which they had been snarlingly withdrawn. His pause was but for a breath or two. Yes, there was no mistaking it. The scent was moose — very far off, but moose, without question. He darted forward at a gallop, but with his muzzle still held high, following that scent up the wind.

Presently he struck the trail of the herd. An

instant's scrutiny told his trained sense that there were calves and young cows, one or another of which he might hope to stampede by his cunning. The same instant's scrutiny revealed to him that the herd had passed nearly an hour ahead of him. Up went the gray cloud of his tail and down went his nose; and then he straightened himself to his top speed, compared to which the pace wherewith he had followed the scent up the wind was a mere casual sauntering.

When he emerged upon the open plateau and reached the spot where the herd had scattered to browse, he slackened his pace and went warily, peering from side to side. The cow-moose, lying down in the bushes to fondle her imprisoned young, was hidden from his sight for the moment; and so it chanced that before he discovered her he came between her and the wind. That scent — it was the taint of death to her. It went through her frame like an electric shock. With a snort of fear and fury she heaved to her feet and stood, wide-eyed and with lowered brow, facing the menace.

The wolf heard that snorting challenge, and saw the awkward bulk of her shoulders as she rose above the scrub. His jaws wrinkled back tightly, baring the full length of his keen white fangs, and a greenish phosphorescent film seemed to pass suddenly across his narrowed eyeballs. But he did not spring at once to the attack. He was surprised. Moreover, he inferred the calf, from the presence of the cow apart from the rest of the herd. And a full-grown cow-moose, with the mother fury in her heart, he knew to be a dangerous adversary. Though she was hornless, he knew the force of her battering front, the swift, sharp stroke of her hoof, the dauntless intrepidity of her courage. Further, though his own courage and the avid urge of his hunger might have led him under other circumstances to attack forthwith, to-night he knew that he must take no chances. The cave in the blue and white rocks was depending on his success. His mate, wounded and heavy with young — if he let himself get disabled in this hunting she must perish miserably. With prudent tactics, therefore, he circled at a safe distance around the hidden pit; and around its rim circled the wary mother, presenting to him ceaselessly the defiance of her huge and sullen front. By this means he easily concluded that the calf was a prisoner in the pit. This being the case, he knew that with patience and his experienced craft the game was safely his. He drew off some half-dozen paces, and sat upon his haunches

CHARLES LIVINGSTON BULL.

contemplatively to weigh the situation. Everything had turned out most fortunately for his hunting, and food would no longer be scarce in the cave of the painted rocks.

III.

That same night, in a cabin of unutterable loneliness some miles to the west of the trail from the moose-yard, a sallow-faced, lean backwoodsman was awakened by the moonlight streaming into his face through the small square window. He glanced at the embers on the open hearth, and knew that for the white maple logs to have so burned down he must have been sleeping a good six hours. And he had turned in soon after the early winter sunset. Rising on his elbow, he threw down the gaudy patchwork quilt of red, yellow, blue, and mottled squares, which draped the bunk in its corner against the rough log walls. He looked long at the thin face of his wife, whose pale brown hair lay over the bare arm crooked beneath her cheek. Her lips looked pathetically white in the decolourising rays which streamed through the window. His mouth, stubbled with a week's growth of dark beard, twitched curiously as he looked. Then he got up, very noiselessly. Stepping across the bare, hard room, whose austerity the moon made more austere, he gazed into a trundle-bed where a yellow-haired, round-faced boy slept, with the chubby sprawling legs and arms of perfect security. The lad's face looked pale to his troubled eyes.

"It's fresh meat they want, the both of 'em," he muttered to himself. "They can't live and thrive on pork an' molasses, nohow!"

His big fingers, clumsily gentle, played for a moment with the child's yellow curls. Then he pulled a thick, gray homespun hunting-shirt over his head, hitched his heavy trousers up under his belt, clothed his feet in three pairs of home-knit socks and heavy cowhide moccasins, took down his rifle, cartridge-pouch, and snowshoes from their nails on the moss-chinked wall, cast one tender look on the sleepers' faces, and slipped out of the cabin door as silently as a shadow.

"I'll have fresh meat for them before next sundown," he vowed to himself.

Outside, amid the chips of his chopping, with a rough well-sweep on one hand and a rougher barn on the other, he knelt to put on his snowshoes. The cabin stood, a desolate, silver-gray dot in the waste of snow, naked to the steely skies of winter. With the curious improvidence of the backwoodsman, he had cut down every tree in the neighbourhood of the cabin, and the thick woods which might so well have sheltered him stood acres distant on every side. When he had settled the thongs of his snowshoes over his moccasins quite to his satisfaction, he straightened himself with a deep breath, pulled his cap well down over his ears, slung his rifle over his shoulder, and started out with the white moon in his face.

In the ancient forest, among the silent wilderness folk, things happen with the slow inexorableness of time. For days, for weeks, nothing may befall. Hour may tread noiselessly on hour, apparently working no change; yet all the time the forces are assembling, and at last doom strikes. The violence is swift, and soon done. And then the great, still world looks inscrutable, unhurried, changeless as before.

So, after long tranquillity, the forces of fate were assembling about that high plateau in the wilderness. The backwoodsman could no longer endure to see the woman and boy pining for the tonic, vitalising juices of fresh meat. He was not a professional hunter. Absorbed in the clearing and securing of a farm in the free forest, he cared not to kill for the killing's sake. For his own part, he was well content with his salt pork, beans and molasses, and corn-meal mush; but when occasion called, he could handle a rifle as backwoodsmen should. On this night, he was all hunter, and his quiet, wide-open eye, alert for every woodland sign, had a fire in it that would have looked strange to the wife and child.

His long strides carried him swiftly through the glimmering glades. Journeying to the north of east, as the gray wolf had to the north of west, he too, before long, struck the trail of the moose, but at a point far beyond that at which the wolf had come upon it. So trampled and confused a trail it was, however, that for a time he took no note of the light wolf track among the heavy footprints of the moose. Suddenly it caught his eye — one print on a smooth spread of snow, emphasised in a pour of unobstructed radiance. He stopped, scrutinised the trail minutely to assure himself he had but a single wolf to deal with, then resumed his march with new zest and springier pace. Hunting was not without its relish for him when it admitted some savour of the combat.

The cabin stood in the valley lands just back of the high plateau, and so it chanced that the backwoodsman had not far to travel that night. Where the trail broke into the open, he stopped, and reconnoitred cautiously through a screen of hemlock boughs. He saw the big gray wolf sitting straight up on his haunches, his tongue hanging out, contemplating securely his intended prey. He saw the dark shape of the cow-moose, obstinately confronting her foe, her hindquarters backed close up to the edge of the gully. He caught the fierce and anxious gleam of her eyes, as she rolled them backward for an instant's reassuring glance at her young one. And, though he could not see the calf in its prisoning pit, he understood the whole situation.

Well, there was a bounty on wolf-snouts, and this fellow's pelt was worth considering. As for the moose, he knew that not a broadside of cannon would scare her away from that hole in the rocks so long as the calf was in it. He took careful aim from his covert. At the report the wolf shot into the air, straightened out, and fell upon the snow, kicking dumbly, a bullet through his neck. As the light faded from his fierce eyes, with it faded out a vision of the cave in the painted rocks. In half a minute he lay still; and the cow-moose, startled by his convulsive leaps more than by the rifle-shot, blew and snorted, eyeing him with new suspicion. Her spacious flank was toward the hunter. He, with cool but hasty fingers, slipped a fresh cartridge into the breech, and aimed with care at a spot low down behind the fore-shoulder.

Again rang out the thin, vicious report, slapping the great silences in the face. The woodsman's aim was true. With a cough the moose fell forward on her knees. Then, with a mighty, shuddering effort, she got up, turned about, and fell again with her head over the edge of the crevice. Her awkward muzzle touched and twitched against the neck of the frightened calf, and with a heavy sigh she lay still.

The settler stepped out from his hiding-place, and examined with deep satisfaction the results of his night's hunting. Already he saw the colour coming back into the pale cheeks of the woman and the child. The wolf's pelt and snout, too, he thought to himself, would get them both some little things they'd like, from the cross-roads store, next time he went in for corn-meal. Then, there was the calf — no meat like moose-veal, after all. He drew his knife from its sheath. But, no; he hated butchering. He slipped the knife back, reloaded his rifle, stepped to the side of the pit, and stood looking down at the baby captive, where it leaned nosing in piteous bewilderment at the head of its dead mother.

Again the woodsman changed his mind. He bit off a chew of black tobacco, and for some moments stood deliberating, stubbly chin in hand. "I'll save him for the boy to play with and bring up," he at last decided.

THE HOMESICKNESS OF KEHONKA

The Homesickness of Kehonka

THE April night, softly chill and full of the sense of thaw, was closing down over the wide salt marshes. Near at hand the waters of the Tantramar, resting at full tide, glimmered through the dusk and lapped faintly among the winter-ruined remnants of the sedge. Far off — infinitely far it seemed in that illusive atmosphere, which was clear, yet full of the ghosts of rain — the last of daylight lay in a thin streak, pale and sharp, along a vast arc of the horizon. Overhead it was quite dark; for there was no moon, and the tenuous spring clouds were sufficient to shut out the stars. They clung in mid-heaven, but kept to their shadowy ranks without descending to obscure the lower air. Space and mystery, mystery and space, lay abroad upon the vague levels of marsh and tide.

Presently, from far along the dark heights of the sky, came voices, hollow, musical, confused. Swiftly they journeyed nearer; they grew louder.

The sound — not vibrant, yet strangely far-carrying — was a clamorous monotony of honk-a-honk, honk-a-honk, honka, honka, honk, honk. It hinted of wide distance voyaged over on tireless wings, of a tropic winter passed in feeding amid remote, high-watered meadows of Mexico and Texas, of long flights yet to go, toward the rocky tarns of Labrador and the reed beds of Ungava. As the sound passed straight overhead the listener on the marsh below imagined, though he could not see, the strongly beating wings, the outstretched necks and heads, the round, unswerving eyes of the wild goose flock in its V-shaped array, winnowing steadily northward through the night. But this particular flock was not set, as it chanced, upon an all-night journey. The wise old gander winging at the head of the V knew of good feeding-grounds near by, which he was ready to revisit. He led the flock straight on, above the many windings of the Tantramar, till its full-flooded sheen far below him narrowed and narrowed to a mere brook. Here, in the neighbourhood of the uplands, were a number of shallow, weedy, fresh-water lakes, with shores so choked with thickets and fenced apart with bogs as to afford a security which his years and broad experience had taught him to value.

Into one of these lakes, a pale blur amid the thick shadows of the shores, the flock dropped with heavy splashings. A scream or two of full-throated content, a few flappings of wings and rufflings of plumage in the cool, and the voyagers settled into quiet.

All night there was silence around the flock, save for the whispering seepage of the snow patches that still lingered among the thickets. With the first creeping pallor of dawn the geese began to feed, plunging their long black necks deep into the water and feeling with the sensitive inner edges of their bills for the swelling root-buds of weed and sedge. When the sun was about the edge of the horizon, and the first rays came sparkling, of a chilly pink most luminous and pure, through the lean traceries of the brushwood, the leader raised his head high and screamed a signal. With answering cries and a tempestuous splashing the flock flapped for a few yards along the surface of the water. Then they rose clear, formed quickly into rank, and in their spacious V went honking northward over the half-lighted, mysterious landscape. But, as it chanced, not all of the flock set out with that morning departure. There was one pair, last year's birds, upon whom had fallen a weariness of travel. Perhaps in the coils of their brains lurked some inherited memory of these safe resting-places and secluded feeding-grounds of the Midgic lakes. However that may have been, they chose to stay where they were, feeling in their blood no call from the cold north solitudes. Dipping and bowing, black neck by neck, they gave no heed to the leader's signal, nor to the noisy going of the flock. Pushing briskly with the black webs of their feet against the discoloured water, they swam to the shore and cast about for a place to build their nest.

There was no urgent hurry, so they chose not on that day nor the next. When they chose, it was a little bushy islet off a point of land, well tangled with alder and osier and a light flotsam of driftwood. The nest, in the heart of the tangle, was an apparently haphazard collection of sticks and twigs, well raised above the damp, well lined with moss and feathers. Here, in course of days, there accumulated a shining cluster of six large white eggs. But by this time the spring freshet had gone down. The islet was an islet no longer, but a mere adjunct of the point, which any inquisitive foot might reach dry shod. Now just at this time it happened that a young farmer, who had a curious taste for all the wild kindred of wood, and flood, and air, came up from the Lower Tantramar with a wagon-load of grist for the Midgic mill. While his buckwheat and barley were a-grinding, he thought of a current opinion to the effect that the wild geese were given to nesting in the Midgic lakes. "If so," said he to himself, "this is the time they would be about it." Full of interest, a half-hour's tramp through difficult woods brought him to the nearest of the waters. An instinct, an intuition born of his sympathy with the furtive folk, led him to the point, and out along the point to that once islet, with its secret in the heart of the tangle. Vain were the furious hissings, the opposing wings, the wide black bills that threatened and oppugned him. With the eager delight of a boy he pounced upon those six great eggs, and carried them all away. "They will soon turn out another clutch," said he to himself, as he left the bereaved pair, and tramped elatedly back to the mill. As for the bereaved pair, being of a philosophic spirit, they set themselves to fulfil as soon as possible his prophecy.

On the farm by the Lower Tantramar, in a hogshead half filled with straw and laid on its side in a dark corner of the tool-shed, those six eggs were diligently brooded for four weeks and two days by a comfortable gray and white goose of the common stock. When they hatched, the good gray and white mother may have been surprised to find her goslings of an olive green hue, instead of the bright golden yellow which her past experience and that of her fellows had taught her to expect. She may have marvelled, too, at their unwonted slenderness and activity. These trivial details, however, in no way dampened the zeal with which she led them to the goose pond, or the fidelity with which she pastured and protected them. But rats, skunks, sundry obscure ailments, and the heavy wheels of the farm wagon, are among the perils which, the summer through, lie in wait for all the children of the feathered kin upon the farm; and so it came about that of the six young ones so successfully hatched from the wild goose eggs, only two lived till the coming of autumn brought them full plumage and the power of flight. Before the time of the southward migration came near, the young farmer took these two and clipped from each the strong primaries of their right wings. "They seem contented enough, and tame as any," he said to himself, "but you never can tell what'll happen when the instinct strikes 'em."

Both the young wild geese were fine males. Their heads and long, slim necks were black, as were also their tails, great wing feathers, bills, and feet. Under the tail their feathers were of snowiest white, and all the other portions of their bodies a rich grayish brown. Each bore on the side of its face a sharply defined triangular patch of white, mottled with faint brown markings that would disappear after his first moult. In one the white cheek patches met under the throat. This was a large, strongly built bird, of a placid and domestic temper. He was satisfied with the undistinguished gray companions of the flock. He was content, like them, to gutter noisily with his discriminating bill along the shallow edges of the pond, to float and dive and flap in the deeper centre, to pasture at random over the wet meadow, biting off the short grasses with quick, sharp, yet gracefully curving dabs. Goose pond and wet meadow and cattle-trodden barnyard bounded his aspirations. When his adult voice came to him, all he would say was honk, honk, contemplatively, and sometimes honk-a-honk when he flapped his wings in the exhilarating coolness of the sunrise. The other captive was of a more restless temperament, slenderer in build, more eager and alert of eye, less companionable of mood. He was, somehow, never seen in the centre of the flock — he never seemed a part of it. He fed, swam, rested, preened himself, always a little apart. Often, when the others were happily occupied with their familiar needs and satisfactions, he would stand motionless, his compact, glossy head high in air, looking to the north as if in expectation, listening as if he awaited longed-for tidings. The triangular white patch on each side of his head was very narrow, and gave him an expression of wildness; yet in reality he was no more wild, or rather no more shy, than any others of the flock. None, indeed, had so confident a fearlessness as he. He would take oats out of the farmer's hand, which none of the rest quite dared to do.

Until late in the autumn, the lonely, uncomraded bird was always silent. But when the migrating flocks began to pass overhead, on the long southward trail, and their hollow clamour was heard over the farmstead night and morning, he grew more restless. He would take a short run with outspread wings, and then, feeling their crippled inefficiency, would stretch himself to his full height and call, a sonorous, far-reaching cry — ke-honk-a, ke-honk-a. From this call, so often repeated throughout October and November, the farmer named him Kehonka. The farmer's wife favoured the more domesticated and manageable brother, who could be trusted

"HE WOULD STAND MOTIONLESS, HIS COMPACT, GLOSSY HEAD HIGH IN AIR."

never to stray. But the farmer, who mused deeply over his furrows, and half wistfully loved the wild kindred, loved Kehonka, and used to say he would not lose the bird for the price of a steer. "That there bird," he would say, "has got dreams away down in his heart. Like as not, he remembers things his father and mother have seen, up amongst the ice cakes and the northern lights, or down amongst the bayous and the big southern lilies." But all his sympathy failed to make him repent of having clipped Kehonka's wing.

During the long winter, when the winds swept fiercely the open marshes of the Tantramar, and the snow piled in high drifts around the barns and wood piles, and the sheds were darkened, and in the sun at noonday the strawy dungheaps steamed, the rest of the geese remained listlessly content. But not so Kehonka. Somewhere back of his brain he cherished pre-natal memories of warm pools in the South, where leafy screens grew rank, and the sweet-rooted water-plants pulled easily from the deep black mud, and his true kindred were screaming to each other at the oncoming of the tropic dark. While the flock was out in the barnyard, pulling lazily at the trampled litter, and snatching scraps of the cattle's chopped turnips, Kehonka would stand aloof by the water-trough, his head erect, listening, longing. As the winter sun sank early over the fir woods back of the farm, his wings would open, and his desirous cry would go echoing three or four times across the still countryside — ke-honk-a — ke-honk-a — ke-honk-a! Whereat the farmer's wife, turning her buckwheat pancakes over the hot kitchen stove, would mutter impatiently; but the farmer, slipping to the door of the cow-stable with the bucket of feed in his hand, would look with deep eyes of sympathy at the unsatisfied bird. "He wants something that we don't grow round here," he would say to himself; and little by little the bird's restlessness came to seem to him the concrete embodiment of certain dim outreachings of his own. He, too, caught himself straining his gaze beyond the marsh horizons of Tantramar.

When the winter broke, and the seeping drifts shrank together, and the brown of the ploughed fields came through the snow in patches, and the slopes leading down to the marshland were suddenly loud with running water, Kehonka's restlessness grew so eager that he almost forgot to feed. It was time, he thought, for the northward flight to begin. He would stand for hours, turning first one dark eye, then the other, toward the soft sky overhead, expectant of the V-shaped journeying flock, and the far-off clamour of voices from the South crying to him in his own tongue. At last, when the snow was about gone from the open fields, one evening at the shutting-in of dark, the voices came. He was lingering at the edge of the goose pond, the rest having settled themselves for the night, when he heard the expected sounds. Honk-a-honk, honk-a-honk, honka, honka, honk, honk, they came up against the light April wind, nearer, nearer, nearer. Even his keen eye could not detect them against the blackness; but up went his wings, and again and again he screamed to them sonorously. In response to his call, their flight swung lower, and the confusion of their honking seemed as if it were going to descend about him. But the wary old gander, their leader, discerned the roofs, man's handiwork, and suspected treachery. At his sharp signal the flock, rising again, streamed off swiftly toward safer feeding-grounds, and left Kehonka to call and call unanswered. Up to this moment all his restlessness had not led him to think of actually deserting the farmstead and the alien flock. Though not of them he had felt it necessary to be with them. His instinct for other scenes and another fellowship had been too little tangible to move him to the snapping of established ties. But now, all his desires at once took concrete form. It was his, it belonged to himself — that strong, free flight, that calling through the sky, that voyaging northward to secret nesting-places. In that wild flock which had for a moment swerved downward to his summons, or in some other flock, was his mate. It was mating season, and not until now had he known it.

Nature does sometimes, under the pressure of great and concentrated desires, make unexpected effort to meet unforeseen demands. All winter long, though it was not the season for such growth, Kehonka's clipped wing-primaries had been striving to develop. They had now, contrary to all custom, attained to an inch or so of effective flying web. Kehonka's heart was near bursting with his desire as the voices of the unseen flock died away. He spread his wings to their full extent, ran some ten paces along the ground, and then, with all his energies concentrated to the effort, he rose into the air, and flew with swift-beating wings out into the dark upon the northward trail. His trouble was not the lack of wing surface, but the lack of balance. One wing being so much less in spread than the other, he felt a fierce force striving to turn him over at every stroke. It was the struggle to counteract this tendency that wore him out. His first desperate effort carried him half a mile. Then he dropped to earth, in a bed of withered salt-grass all awash with the full tide of Tantramar. Resting amid the salt-grass, he tasted such an exultation of freedom that his heart forgot its soreness over the flock which had vanished. Presently, however, he heard again the sound that so thrilled his every vein. Weird, hollow, echoing with memories and tidings, it came throbbing up the wind. His own strong cry went out at once to meet it — ke-honk-a, ke-honk-a, ke-honk-a. The voyagers this time were flying very low. They came near, nearer, and at last, in a sudden silence of voices, but a great flapping of wings, they settled down in the salt-grass all about him.

The place was well enough for a night's halt — a shallow, marshy pool which caught the overflow of the highest spring tides, and so was not emptied by the ebb. After its first splashing descent into the water, which glimmered in pale patches among the grass stems, every member of the flock sat for some moments motionless as statues, watchful for unknown menace; and Kehonka, his very soul trembling with desire achieved, sat motionless among them. Then, there being no sign of peril at hand, there was a time of quiet paddling to and fro, a scuttling of practised bills among the grass-roots, and Kehonka found himself easily accepted as a member of the flock. Happiness kept him restless and on the move long after the others had their bills tucked under their wings. In the earliest gray of dawn, when the flock awoke to feed, Kehonka fed among them as if he had been with them all the way on their flight from the Mexican plains. But his feeding was always by the side of a young female who had not yet paired. It was interrupted by many little courtesies of touching bill and bowing head, which were received with plain favour; for Kehonka was a handsome and well marked bird. By the time the sky was red along the east and strewn with pale, blown feathers of amber pink toward the zenith, his swift wooing was next door to winning. He had forgotten his captivity and clipped wing. He was thinking of a nest in the wide emptiness of the North.

When the signal-cry came, and the flock took flight, Kehonka rose with them. But his preliminary rush along the water was longer than that of the others, and when the flock formed into flying order he fell in at the end of the longer leg of the

"FELL WITH A GREAT SPLASH INTO THE CHANNEL OF THE

V, behind the weakest of the young geese. This would have been a humiliation to him, had he taken thought of it at all; but his attention was all absorbed in keeping his balance. When the flock found its pace, and the cold sunrise air began to whistle past the straight, bullet-like rush of their flight, a terror grew upon him. He flew much better than he had flown the night before; but he soon saw that this speed of theirs was beyond him. He would not yield, however. He would not lag behind. Every force of his body and his brain went into that flight, till his eyes blurred and his heart seemed on the point of bursting. Then, suddenly, with a faint, despairing note, he lurched aside, shot downward, and fell with a great splash into the channel of the Tantramar. With strong wings, and level, unpausing flight, the flock went on to its North without him.

Dazed by the fall, and exhausted by the intensity of his effort, Kehonka floated, moveless, for many minutes. The flood-tide, however, racing inland, was carrying him still northward; and presently he began to swim in the same direction. In his sick heart glowed still the vision of the nest in the far-off solitudes, and he felt that he would find there, waiting for him, the strong-winged mate who had left him behind. Half an hour later another flock passed honking overhead, and he called to them; but they were high up, and feeding time was past. They gave no sign in answer. He made no attempt to fly after them. Hour after hour he swam on with the current, working ever north. When the tide turned he went ashore, still following the river, till its course changed toward the east; whereupon he ascended the channel of a small tributary which flowed in on the north bank. Here and there he snatched quick mouthfuls of sprouting grasses, but he was too driven by his desire to pause for food. Sometimes he tried his wings again, covering now some miles at each flight, till by and by, losing the stream because its direction failed him, he found himself in a broken upland country, where progress was slow and toilsome. Soon after sunset, troubled because there was no water near, he again took wing, and over dark woods which filled him with apprehension he made his longest flight. When about spent he caught a small gleaming of water far below him, and alighted in a little woodland glade wherein a brook had overflowed low banks.

The noise of his abrupt descent loudly startled the wet and dreaming woods. It was a matter of interest to all the furry, furtive ears of the forest

"THE DISCOURAGER OF QUESTS DARTED STEALTHILY FORTH."

for a half-mile round. But it was in no way repeated. For perhaps fifteen minutes Kehonka floated, neck erect, head high and watchful, in the middle of the pool, with no movement except the slight, unseen oaring of his black-webbed feet, necessary to keep the current from bearing him into the gloom of the woods. This gloom, hedging him on every side, troubled him with a vague fear. But in the open of the mid-pool, with two or three stars peering faintly through the misted sky above him, he felt comparatively safe. At last, very far above, he heard again that wild calling of his fellows,— honk-a-honk, honk-a-honk, honka, honka, honk, honk.— high and dim and ghostly, for these rough woodlands had no appeal for the journeying flocks. Remote as the voices were, however, Kehonka answered at once. His keen, sonorous, passionate cry rang strangely on the night, three times. The flock paid no heed to it whatever, but sped on northward with unvarying flight and clamour; and as the wizard noise passed beyond, Kehonka, too weary to take wing, followed eagerly to the northerly shore of the pool, ran up the wet bank, and stood straining after it.

His wings were half spread as he stood there, quivering with his passion. In his heart was the hunger of the quest. In his eyes was the vision of nest and mate, where the serviceberry thicket grew by the wide sub-arctic waters. The night wind blew steadily away from him to the underbrush close by, or even in his absorption he would have noticed the approach of a menacing, musky smell. But every sense was now numb in the presence of his great desire. There was no warning for him.

The underbrush rustled, ever so softly. Then a small, delicately moving, fine-furred shape, the discourager of quests, darted stealthily forth, and with a bound that was feathery in its blown lightness, seeming to be uplifted by the wide-plumed tail that balanced it, descended on Kehonka's body. There was a thin honk, cut short by keen teeth meeting with a crunch and a twist in the glossy slim blackness of Kehonka's neck. The struggle lasted scarcely more than two heart-beats. The wide wings pounded twice or thrice upon the ground, in fierce convulsion. Then the red fox, with a sidewise jerk of his head, flung the heavy, trailing carcass into a position for its easy carrying, and trotted off with it into the darkness of the woods.

SAVOURY MEATS

Savoury Meats

IN the bushy thicket the doe stood trembling over the young one to which she had given birth in the early part of the night. A light wind began to breathe just before dawn, and in its languid throbbing the slim twigs and half unfolded leaves from time to time rustled stiffly. Over the tree-tops, and from the open spaces in the wood, could be seen the first pallor of approaching day; and one pink thread, a finger long, outlined a lonely fragment of the horizon. But in the bushy thicket it was dark. The mother could not see her little one, but kept feeling it anxiously and lightly with her silken nose. She was waiting till it should be strong enough to rise and nurse.

As the pink thread became scarlet and crept along a wider arc, and the cold light spread, there came from a far-off hillside the trailing echo of a howl. It was the cry of a wolf hunting alone. It hardly penetrated the depths of the bushy thicket but the doe heard it, and faced about to the point whence it came, and stamped angrily with slim, sharp hoof. Her muzzle was held high, and her nostrils expanded tensely, weighing and analysing every scent that came on the chill air. But the dread cry was not repeated. No smell of danger breathed in her retreat. The light stole at last through the tangled branches. Then the little one struggled to its feet, its spotted sides still heaving under the stress of their new expansion; and the doe, with lowered head and neck bent far around, watched it with great eyes as it pressed its groping mouth against her udder and learned to feed.

Presently the sides of branch and stem and leaf facing the dawn took on a hue of pink. A male song-sparrow, not yet feeling quite at home after his journey from the South, sang hesitatingly from the top of a bush. A pair of crows squawked gutturally and confidentially in a tree-top, where they contemplated nesting. Everything was wet, but it was a tonic and stimulating wetness, like that of a vigorous young swimmer climbing joyously out of a cool stream. The air had a sharp savour, a smell of gummy aromatic buds, and sappy twigs, and pungent young leaves. But the body of the scent, which seemed like the very person of spring, was the affluence of the fresh earth, broken and turned up to the air by millions of tiny little thrusting blades. Presently, when the light fell into the thicket with a steeper slant, the doe stepped away, and left her little one lying, hardly to be discerned, on a spotted heap of dead leaves and moss. She stole noiselessly out of the thicket. She was going to pasture on the sprouting grasses of a neighbouring wild meadow, and to drink at the amber stream that bordered it. She knew that, in her absence, the little one's instinct would teach him to keep so still that no marauder's eye would be likely to detect him.

Two or three miles away from the thicket, in the heart of the same deep-wooded wilderness, stood a long, low-roofed log cabin, on the edge of a narrow clearing. The yard was strewn with chips, some fresh cut and some far gone in decay. A lean pig rooted among them, turning up the black soil that lay beneath. An axe and black iron pot stood on the battered step before the door. In the window appeared the face of an old man, gazing blankly out upon the harsh-featured scene.

The room where the old man sat was roughly ceiled and walled with brown boards. The sunlight streamed in the window, showing the red stains of rust on the cracked kitchen stove, and casting an oblong figure of brightness on the faded patchwork quilt which covered the low bed in the corner. Two years earlier John Hackett had been an erect and powerful woodsman, strong in the task of carving himself a home out of the unyielding wilderness. Then his wife had died of a swift consumption. A few weeks later he had been struck down with paralysis, from which he partly recovered to find himself grown suddenly senile and a helpless invalid. On his son, Silas, fell the double task of caring for him and working the scant, half-subjugated farm.

Streaks and twines of yellowish white were scattered thickly amid the ragged blackness of the old man's hair and beard. The strong, gaunt lines of his features consorted strangely with the piteous weakness that now trembled in his eyes and on his lower lip. He sat in a big home-made easy chair, which Silas had constructed for him by sawing a quarter-section out of a hogshead. This rude frame the lad had lined laboriously with straw and coarse sacking, and his father had taken great delight in it.

A soiled quilt of blue, magenta, and white squares wrapped the old man's legs, as he sat by the window

Savoury Meats 147

waiting for Silas to come in. His withered hands picked ceaselessly at the quilt.

"I wish Si'd come! I want my breakfast!" he kept repeating, now wistfully, now fretfully. His gaze wandered from the window to the stove, from the stove to the window, with slow regularity. When the pig came rooting into his line of vision, it vexed him, and he muttered peevishly to himself.

"That there hog'll hev the whole place rooted up. I wish Si'd come and drive him out of that!"

At last Si came. The old man's face smoothed itself, and a loving light came into his eyes as the lad adjusted the pillow at his head. The doings of the hog were forgotten.

Si bustled about to get breakfast, the old man's eyes following every movement. The tea was placed on the back of the stove to draw. A plate of cold buckwheat cakes was brought out of the cupboard and set on the rude table. A cup, with its handle broken off, was half filled with molasses, for "sweetenin'," and placed beside the buckwheat cakes. Then Si cut some thick slices of salt pork and began to fry them. They "sizzled" cheerfully in the pan, and to Si, with his vigorous morning appetite, the odour was rare and fine. But the old man was troubled by it. His hands picked faster at the quilt.

"Si," said he, in a quavering voice, that rose and fell without regard to the force of the words, "I know ye can't help it, but my stomach's turned agin salt pork! It's been a-comin' on me this long while, that I couldn't eat it no more. An' now it's come. Pork, pork, pork, — I can't eat it no more, Si! But there, I know ye can't help it. Ye're a good boy, a kind son, Si, and ye can't help it!"

Si went on turning the slices with an old fork till the quavering voice stopped. Then he cried, cheerfully:

"Try an' eat a leetle mite of it, father. This 'ere tea's *fine,* an'll sort of wash it down. An' while I'm a-working in the back field this morning I'll try and think of somethin' to kinder tickle your appetite!"

The old man shook his head gloomily.

"I can't eat no more fried pork, Si," said he, "not if I die fur it! I know ye can't help it! An' it don't matter, fur I won't be here much longer anyways. It'll be a sight better fur you, Si, when I'm gone — but I kinder don't like to leave ye here all alone. Seems like I kinder keep the house warm fur ye till ye come home! I don't like to think of ye comin' in an' findin' the house all empty, Si! But it's been powerful empty, with jist you an' me, sence mother died. It useter be powerful good, Si, didn't it, comin' home and findin' her a-waitin' fur us, an' hot supper ready on the table, an' the lamp a-shinin' cheerful? An' what suppers she could cook! D'ye mind the pies, an' the stews, an' the fried deer's meat? I could eat some of that fried deer's meat now, Si. An' I feel like it would make me better. It ain't no fault of yours, Si, but I can't eat no more salt pork!"

Si lifted the half-browned slices of yellow and crimson on to a plate, poured the gravy over them, and set the plate on the table. Then he dragged his father's chair over to the table, helped him to tea and buckwheat cakes and molasses, and sat down to his own meal. The fried pork disappeared swiftly in his strong young jaws, while his father nibbled reluctantly at the cold and soggy cakes. Si cleared the table, fed the fire, dragged his father back to the sunny window, and then took down the long gun, with the powder-horn and shot-pouch, which hung on pegs behind the door.

The old man noticed what he was doing.

"Ain't ye goin' to work in the back field, Silas?" he asked, plaintively.

"No, father," said the lad, "I'm goin' a-gunnin'. Ef I don't have some of that fried deer's meat fur your supper to-night, like mother useter fix fur ye, my name ain't Silas Hackett!"

He set a tin of fresh water on the window ledge within reach of his father's hand, gave one tender touch to the pillow, and went out quickly. The old man's eyes strained after him till he disappeared in the woods.

Silas walked with the noiseless speed of the trained woodsman. His heart was big with pity for his father, and heavy with a sense of approaching loss. But instinctively his eyes took note of the new life beginning to surge about him in myriad and tumultuous activity. It surged, too, in the answering current of his strong young blood; and from time to time he would forget his heaviness utterly for a moment, thrilled through and through by a snatch of bird song, or a glimpse of rose-red maple buds, or a gleam of ineffable blueness through the tree-tops, or a strange, clean-smelling wind that made him stop and stretch his lungs to take it in. Suddenly he came upon a fresh deer-track.

The sorcery of spring was forgotten. His heaviness was forgotten. He was now just the hunter, keen upon the trail of the quarry. Bending low, silent as a shadow, peering like a panther, he slipped between the great trunks, and paused in the fringe of downy catkined willows that marked the meadow's edge. On the other side of the meadow he saw the form of a doe, drinking. He heard on the wet air the sharp, chiming brawl of the brook, fretted by some obstruction. He took a careful aim. The doe lifted her head, satisfied, and ready to return to her young one in the thicket. A shot rang out across the meadow, and she sprang into the air, to fall back with her slender muzzle in the stream, her forelegs bent beneath her, her hind legs twitching convulsively for a moment before they stiffened out upon the grass.

As Silas staggered homeward he was no longer the keen hunter. He no longer heard the summons of the spring morning. All he thought of was the pleasure which would light up the wan and piteous face of the old man in the chair by the window when the savoury smell of the frying deer's meat would fill the dusky air of the cabin. As he crossed the chip-strewn yard, he saw his father's face watching for him. He dropped his burden at the door, and entered, panting and triumphant.

"I've got it fur ye, father!" he cried, softly touching the tremulous hands with his big brown fingers.

"I'm right glad, Si," quavered the old man, "but

I'm a sight gladder to see ye back! The hours is long when ye're not by me! Oh, but ye do mind me of your mother, Si!"

Si took the carcass to the shed, dressed it carefully, and then, after cutting several thick slices from the haunch, stowed it in the little black hole of a cellar, beneath the cabin floor. He put some fair potatoes to boil, and proceeded to fry the juicy steaks which the old man loved. The fragrance of them filled the cabin. The old man's eyes grew brighter, and his hands less tremulous. When the smoking and sputtering dish was set upon the table, Silas again drew up the big chair, and the two made a joyous meal. The old man ate as he had not eaten for months, and the generous warmth of the fresh meat put new life into his withered veins. His under lip grew firmer, his voice steadier, his brain more clear. With a gladness that brought tears into his eyes, Silas marked the change.

"Father," he cried, "ye look more like yerself than I've seen ye these two years past!"

And the old man replied, with a ring of returning hope in his voice:

"This 'ere deer's meat's more'n any medicine. Ef I git well, ever, seems to me it'll be according to what I eat or don't eat, more'n anything else."

"TWO GREEN EYES ... LOOKED AT HIM."

"Whatever ye think'll help ye, that ye shall hev, father," declared Silas, "ef I have to crawl on hands an' knees all day an' all night fur it!"

Meanwhile, in the heart of the bushy thicket, on the spotted heap of leaves, lay a little fawn, waiting for its mother. It was trembling now with hunger and chill. But its instinct kept it silent all day long. The afternoon light died out. Twilight brought a bitter chill to the depths of the thicket. When night came, hunger, cold, and fear at last overcame the little one's muteness. From time to time it gave a plaintive cry, then waited, and listened for its mother's coming. The cry was feeble, but there were keen ears in the forest to catch it. There came a stealthy crackling in the bushes, and the fawn struggled to its feet with a glad expectation. Two green eyes, close to the ground, floated near. There was a pounce, a scuffle — and then the soft, fierce whispering sound of a wildcat satisfying itself with blood.

THE BOY AND HUSHWING

The Boy and Hushwing

A HOLLOW, booming, ominous cry, a great voice of shadowy doom, rang out suddenly and startled the dark edges of the forest. It sounded across the glimmering pastures, vibrating the brown-violet dusk, and made the lame old woman in the cabin on the other side of the clearing shiver with vague fears.

But not vague was the fear which shook the soul of the red squirrel where he crouched, still for once in his restless life, in the crotch of a thick spruce-top. Not vague was the fear of the brooding grouse in the far-off withe-wood thicket, though the sound came to her but dimly and she knew that the menace of it was not, at the moment, for her. And least vague of all was the terror of the usually unterrified weasel, from whose cruel little eyes the red flame of the blood-lust faded suddenly, as the glow dies out of a coal; for the dread voice sounded very close to him, and it required all his nerve to hold himself rigidly motionless and to refrain from the start which would have betrayed him to his death.

"*Whoo-hoo-oo-h'oo-oo!*" boomed the call again, seeming to come from the tree-tops, the thickets, the sky, and the earth, all at once, so that creatures many hundred yards apart trembled simultaneously, deeming that the clutch of fate was already at their necks. But to the Boy, as he let down the pasture bars with a clatter and turned the new-milked cows in among the twilight-coloured hillocks, the sound brought no terror. He smiled as he said to himself: "There's Hushwing again at his hunting. I must give him a taste of what it feels like to be hunted." Then he strolled across the pasture, between the black stumps, the blueberry patches, the tangles of wild raspberry; pushed softly through the fringe of wild cherry and young birch saplings, and crept, soundless as a snake, under the branches of a low-growing hemlock. Peering out from this covert he could see, rising solitary at the back of an open glade, the pale and naked trunk of a pine-tree, which the lightning had shattered.

The Boy's eyes were keen as a fish-hawk's, and he kept them fixed upon the top of the pine trunk. Presently it seemed as if the spirit of the dusk took shadowy form for an instant. There was a soundless sweeping of wings down the glade, and the next moment the pine trunk looked about two feet taller in the Boy's eyes. The great horned owl — "Hushwing," the Boy had christened him, for the ghostly silence of his flight — had returned to his favourite post of observation, whereon he stood so erect and motionless that he seemed a portion of the pine trunk itself.

The Boy lay still as a watching lynx, being minded to spy on Hushwing at his hunting. A moment more, and then came again that hollow summons: *W'hoo-hoo-hoo-who'o-oo;* and the great owl turned his head to listen as the echo floated through the forest.

The Boy heard, a few paces distant from him, the snap of a twig where a startled hare stirred clumsily. The sound was faint; indeed so faint that he was hardly sure whether he heard or imagined it; but to the wonderfully wide and sensitive drum of the owl's ear it sounded sharply away down at the foot of the glade. Ere the Boy could draw a second breath he saw great wings hovering at the edge of the thicket close at hand. He saw big, clutching talons outstretched from thick-feathered legs, while round eyes, fiercely gleaming, flamed upon his in passing as they searched the bush. Once the great wings backed off, foiled by some obstruction which the Boy could not see. Then they pounced with incredible speed. There was a flapping and a scuffle, followed by a loud squeak; and Hushwing winnowed off down the glade bearing the limp form of the hare in his talons. He did not stop at the pine trunk, but passed on toward the deeper woods.

"He's got a mate and a nest 'way back in the cedar swamp, likely," said the Boy, as he got up, stretched his cramped limbs, and turned his face homeward. As he went, he schemed with subtle woodcraft for the capture of the wary old bird. He felt impelled to try his skill against the marauder's inherited cunning and suspicion; and he knew that, if he should succeed, there would remain Hushwing's yet fiercer and stronger mate to care for the little owlets in the nest.

When Hushwing had deposited his prey beside the nest, in readiness for the next meal of his ever-hungry nestlings, he sailed off again for a hunt on his own account. Now it chanced that a rare visitor, a wanderer from the cliffy hills which lay many miles back of Hushwing's cedar swamp, had come down that day to see if there might not be a sheep or a calf to be picked up on the outskirts of the settlements. It was years since a panther had been seen in that neighbourhood — it was years, indeed, since that particular panther had strayed from his high fastnesses, where game was plentiful and none dared poach on his preserves. But just now a camp of hunters on his range had troubled him seriously and scattered his game. Gnawing his heart with rage and fear, he had succeeded so far in evading their noisy search, and had finally come to seek vengeance by taking tribute of their flocks. He had traversed the cedar swamp, and emerging upon the wooded uplands he had come across a cow-path leading down to the trampled brink of a pond.

"Here," he thought to himself, "will the cattle come to drink, and I will kill me a yearling heifer." On the massive horizontal limb of a willow which overhung the trodden mire of the margin he stretched himself to await the coming of the quarry. A thick-leaved beech bough, thrusting in among the willow branches, effectually concealed him. Only from above was he at all visible, his furry ears and the crown of his head just showing over the leafage.

The aerial path of Hushwing, from his nest in the swamp to his watch-tower on the clearing's edge, led him past the pool and the crouching panther. He had never seen a panther, and he had nothing in his brain-furnishing to fit so formidable a beast. On chance, thinking perhaps to strike a mink at his fishing on the pool's brink, he sounded his *Whoo-hoo-hoo-who'o-oo!* as he came near. The panther turned his head at the sound, rustling the leaves, over which appeared his furry ear-tips. The next instant, to his rage and astonishment, he received a smart blow on the top of his head, and sharp claws tore the tender skin about his ears. With a startled snarl he turned and struck upward with his armed paw, a lightning stroke, at the unseen assailant.

But he struck the empty air. Already was Hushwing far on his way, a gliding ghost. He was puzzled over the strange animal which he had struck; but while his wits were yet wondering, those miracles of sensitiveness, those living telephone films which served him for ears, caught the scratching of light claws on the dry bark of a hemlock some ten paces aside from his line of flight. Thought itself could hardly be more silent and swift than was his turning. The next moment his noiseless wings overhung a red squirrel, where it lay flattened to the bark in the crotch of the hemlock. Some dream of the hunt or the flight had awakened the little

"HE STRUCK THE EMPTY AIR."

animal to an unseasonable activity and betrayed it to its doom. There was a shrill squeal as those knife-like talons met in the small, furry body; then Hushwing carried off his supper to be eaten comfortably upon his watch-tower.

Meanwhile the Boy was planning the capture of the wise old owl. He might have shot the bird easily, but wanton slaughter was not his object, and he was no partisan as far as the wild creatures were concerned. All the furtive folk, fur and feather alike, were interesting to him, even dear to him in varying degrees. He had no grudge against Hushwing for his slaughter of the harmless hare and grouse, for did not the big marauder show equal zest in the pursuit of mink and weasel, snake and rat? Even toward that embodied death, the malignant weasel, indeed, the Boy had no antagonism, making allowance as he did for the inherited blood-lust which drove the murderous little animal to defy all the laws of the wild kindred and kill, kill, kill, for the sheer delight of killing. The Boy's purpose now in planning the capture of Hushwing was, first of all, to test his own woodcraft; and, second, to get the bird under his close observation. He had a theory that the big horned owl might be tamed so as to become an interesting and highly instructive pet. In any case, he was sure that Hushwing in captivity might be made to contribute much to his knowledge,—and knowledge, first-hand knowledge, of all the furtive kindred of the wild, knowledge such as the text-books on natural history which his father's library contained could not give him, was what he continually craved.

On the following afternoon the Boy went early to the neighbourhood of Hushwing's watch-tower. At the edge of a thicket, half concealed, but open toward the dead pine trunk, was a straggling colony of low blueberry bushes. Where the blueberry bushes rose some eight or ten inches above the top of a decaying birch stump he fixed a snare of rabbit wire. To the noose he gave a diameter of about a foot, supporting it horizontally in the tops of the bushes just over the stump. The cord from the noose he carried to his hiding-place of the previous evening, under the thick-growing hemlock. Then he went home, did up some chores upon which he depended for his pocket-money, and arranged with the hired man to relieve him for that evening of his duty of driving the cows back to pasture after the milking. Just before the afternoon began to turn from brown amber to rose and lilac he went back to the glade of the pine trunk. This time he took with him the body of one of the big gray rats which infested his father's grain-bins. The rat he fixed securely upon the top of the stump among the blueberry bushes, exactly under the centre of the snare. Then he broke off the tops of a berry bush, tied the stubs together loosely, drew them over, ran the string once around the stump, and carried the end of the string back to his hiding-place beside the cord of the snare. Pulling the string gently, he smiled with satisfaction to hear the broken twigs scratch seductively on the stump, like the claws of a small animal. Then he lay down, both cords in his hand, and composed himself to a season of patient waiting.

He had not long to wait, however; for Hushwing was early at his hunting that night. The Boy turned away his scrutiny for just one moment, as it seemed to him; but when he looked again there was Hushwing at his post, erect, apparently part of the pine trunk. Then — *Whoo-hoo-hoo-who'o-oo!* sounded his hollow challenge, though the sunset colour was not yet fading in the west. Instantly the Boy pulled his string; and from the stump among the blueberry bushes came a gentle scratching, as of claws. Hushwing heard it. Lightly, as if blown on a swift wind, he was at the spot. He struck. His great talons transfixed the rat. His wings beat heavily as he strove to lift it, to bear it off to his nestlings. But what a heavy beast it was, to be sure! The next moment the noose of rabbit wire closed inexorably upon his legs. He loosed his grip upon the rat and sprang into the air, bewildered and terrified. But his wings would not bear him the way he wished to go. Instead, a strange, irresistible force was drawing him, for all the windy beating of his pinions, straight to an unseen doom in the heart of a dense-growing hemlock.

A moment more and he understood his discomfiture and the completeness of it. The Boy stood forth from his hiding-place, grinning; and Hushwing knew that his fate was wholly in the hands of this master being, whom no wild thing dared to hunt. Courageous to the last, he hissed fiercely and snapped his sharp beak in defiance; but the Boy drew him down, muffled wing, beak, and talons in his heavy homespun jacket, bundled him under his arm, and carried him home in triumph.

"You'll find the rats in our oat-bins," said he, "fatter than any weasel in the wood, my Hushwing."

The oat-bins were in a roomy loft at one end

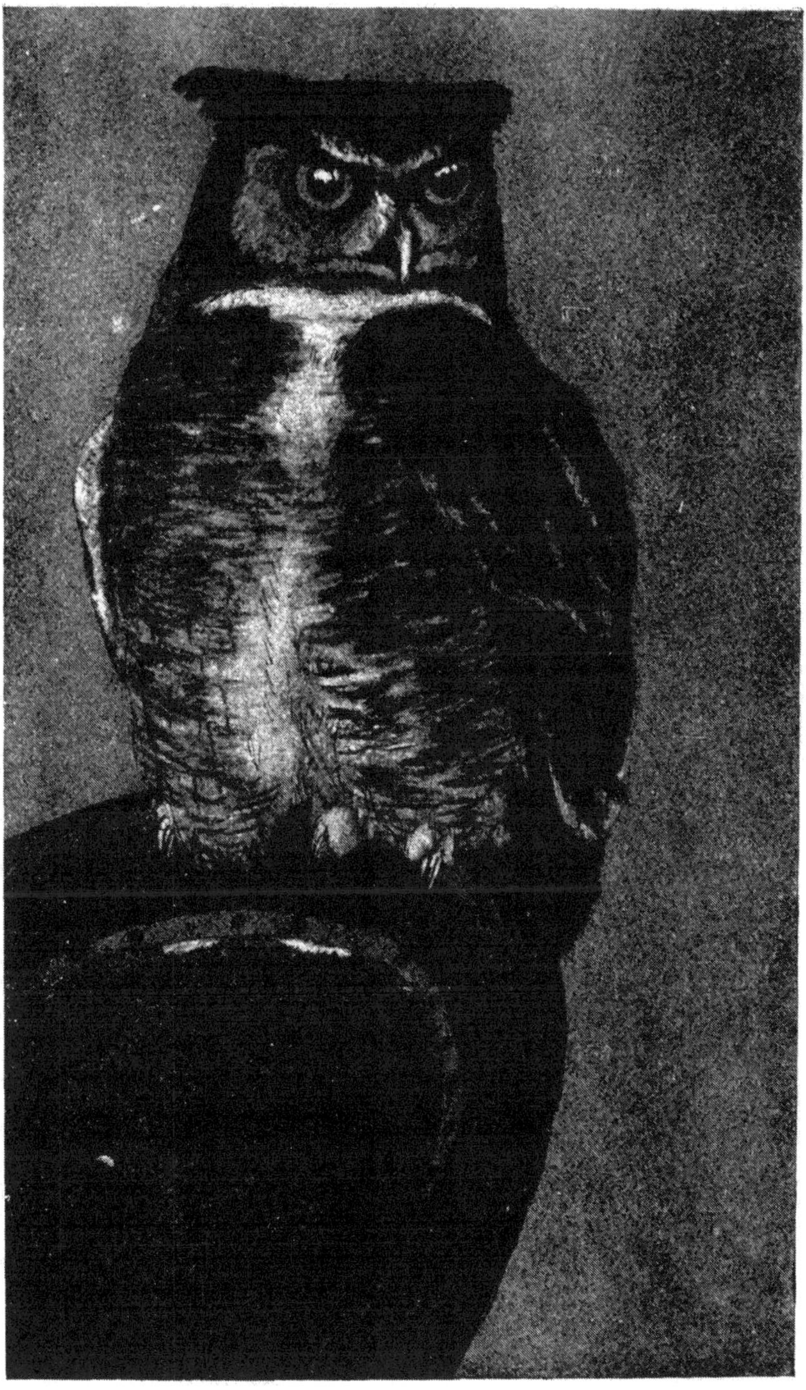

of the wood-shed. The loft was lighted by a large square window in the gable, arranged to swing back on hinges like a door, for convenience in passing the bags of grain in and out. Besides three large oat-bins, it contained a bin for barley, one for buckwheat, and one for bran. The loft was also used as a general storehouse for all sorts of stuff that would not keep well in a damp cellar; and it was a very paradise for rats. From the wood-shed below admittance to the loft was gained by a flight of open board stairs and a spacious trap-door.

Mounting these stairs and lifting the trap-door, the boy carefully undid the wire noose from Hushwing's feathered legs, avoiding the keen talons which promptly clutched at his fingers. Then he unrolled the coat, and the big bird, flapping his wings eagerly, soared straight for the bright square of the window. But the sash was strong; and the glass was a marvel which he had never before encountered. In a few moments he gave up the effort, floated back to the duskiest corner of the loft, and settled himself, much disconcerted, on the back of an old haircloth sofa which had lately been banished from the sitting-room. Here he sat immovable, only hissing and snapping his formidable beak when the Boy approached him. His heart swelled with indignation and despair; and, realising the futility of flight, he stood at bay. As the Boy moved around him he kept turning his great horned head as if it were on a pivot, without changing the position of his body; and his round, golden eyes, with their piercing black pupils, met those of his captor with an unflinching directness beyond the nerve of any four-footed beast, however mighty, to maintain. The daunting mastery of the human gaze, which could prevail over the gaze of the panther or the wolf, was lost upon the tameless spirit of Hushwing. Noting his courage, the Boy smiled approval and left him alone to recover his equanimity.

The Boy, as days went by, made no progress whatever in his acquaintance with his captive, who steadfastly met all his advances with defiance of hissings and snapping beak. But by opening the bins and sitting motionless for an hour or two in the twilight the Boy was able to make pretty careful study of Hushwing's method of hunting. The owl would sit a long time unstirring, the gleam of his eyes never wavering. Then suddenly he would send forth his terrifying cry,—and listen. Sometimes there would be no result. At other times the cry would come just as some big rat, grown over-confident, was venturing softly across the floor or down into the toothsome grain. Startled out of all common sense by that voice of doom at his ear, he would make a desperate rush for cover. There would be a scrambling on the floor or a scurrying in the bin. Then the great, dim wings would hover above the sound. There would be a squeak, a brief scuffle; and Hushwing would float back downily to devour his prey on his chosen perch, the back of the old haircloth sofa.

For a fortnight the Boy watched him assiduously, spending almost every evening in the loft. At length came an evening when not a rat would stir abroad, and Hushwing's hunting-calls were hooted in vain. After two hours of vain watching the Boy's patience gave out, and he went off to bed, promising his prisoner a good breakfast in the morning to compensate him for the selfish prudence of the rats. That same night, while every one in the house slept soundly, it chanced that a thieving squatter from the other end of the settlement came along with a bag, having designs upon the well-filled oat-bins.

The squatter knew where there was a short and handy ladder leaning against the tool-house. He had always been careful to replace it. He also knew how to lift, with his knife, the iron hook which fastened — but did not secure — the gable window on the inside. To-night he went very stealthily, because, though it was dark, there was no wind to cover the sound of his movements. Stealthily he brought the ladder and raised it against the gable of the loft. Noiselessly he mounted, carrying his bag, till his bushy, hatless head was just on a level with the window-sill. Without a sound, as he imagined, his knife-edge raised the hook — but there *was* a sound, the ghost of a sound, and the marvellous ear of Hushwing heard it. As the window swung back the thief's bushy crown appeared just over the sill. "*Whoo-h'oo-oo!*" shouted Hushwing, angry and hungry, swooping at the seductive mark. He struck it fair and hard, his claws gashing the scalp, his wings dealing an amazing buffet.

Appalled by the cry and the stroke, the sharp clutch, the great smother of wing, the rascal screamed with terror, lost his hold, and fell to the ground. Nothing was further from his imagination than that his assailant should be a mere owl. It was rather some kind of a grossly inconsistent hobgoblin that he thought of, sent to punish him for the theft of his neighbour's grain. Leaving the ladder where it fell, and the empty bag beside it, he ran wildly from the haunted spot, and never stopped till he found himself safe inside his shanty door. As for Hushwing, he did not wait to investigate this second mistake of his, but made all haste back to his nest in the swamp.

The frightened outcry of the thief awoke the sleepers in the house, and presently the Boy and his father came with a lantern to find out what was the matter. The fallen ladder, the empty bag, the open window of the loft, told their own story. When the Boy saw that Hushwing was gone, his face fell with disappointment. He had grown very fond of his big, irreconcilable, dauntless captive.

"We owe Master Hushwing a right good turn this night," said the Boy's father, laughing. "My grain's going to last longer after this, I'm thinking."

"Yes," sighed the Boy, "Hushwing has earned his freedom. I suppose I mustn't bother him any more with snares and things."

Meanwhile, the great horned owl was sitting erect on the edge of his nest in the swamp, one talon transfixing the torn carcass of a mink, while his shining eyes, round like little suns, shone happily upon the big-headed, ragged-feathered, hungry brood of owlets at his feet.

A TREASON OF NATURE

A Treason of Nature

THE full moon of October, deep orange in a clear, deep sky, hung large and somewhat distorted just over the wooded hills that rimmed the lake. Through the ancient forest, a mixed growth of cedar, water-ash, black poplar, and maple, with here and there a group of hemlocks on a knoll, the light drained down confusedly, a bewildering chaos of bright patches, lines, and reticulations amid breadths of blackness. On the half-overshadowed cove, which here jutted in from the lake, the mingling of light and darkness wrought an even more elusive mystery than in the wood. For the calm levels just breathed, as it were, with a fading remembrance of the wind which had blown till sundown over the open lake. The pulse of this breathing whimsically shifted the reflections, and caused the pallid water-lily leaves to uplift and appeal like the glimmering hands of ghosts. The stillness was perfect, save for a ceaseless, faintly rhythmic h-r-r-r-r-r-ing, so light that only the most finely attentive ear, concentrated to the effort, might distinguish it. This was the eternal breathing of the ancient wood. In such a silence there was nothing to hint of the thronging, furtive life on every side, playing under the moonlit glamour its uneven game with death. If a twig snapped in the distance, if a sudden rustle somewhere stirred the moss — it might mean love, it might mean the inevitable tragedy.

Under a tall water-ash some rods back from the shore of the cove, there was a sharp, clacking sound, and a movement which caused a huge blur of lights and shadows to differentiate itself all at once into the form of a gigantic bull-moose. The animal had been resting quite motionless till the tickling of some insect at the back of his ear disturbed him. Lowering his head, he lifted a hind leg and scratched the place with sharp strokes of his sprawling, deeply cloven hoof; and the two loose sections of the hoof clacked together between each stroke like castanets. Then he moved a step forward, till his head and fore-shoulders came out into the full illumination of a little lane of moonlight pouring in betweeen the tree-tops.

He was a prince of his kind, as he stood there with long, hooked, semi-prehensile muzzle thrust forward, his nostrils dilating to savour the light airs which drifted almost imperceptibly through the forest. His head, in this attitude, — an attitude of considering watchfulness, — was a little lower than the thin-maned ridge of his shoulders, over which lay back the vast palmated adornment of his antlers. These were like two curiously outlined, hollowed leaves, serrated with some forty prongs; and their tips, at the point of widest expansion, were little less than six feet apart. His eyes, though small for the rough-hewn bulk of his head, were keen, and ardent with passion and high courage. His ears, large and coarse for one of the deer tribe to possess, were set very low on his skull — to such a degree, indeed, as to give somehow a daunting touch of the monstrous to his massive dignity. His neck was short and immensely powerful, to support the gigantic head and antlers. From his throat hung a strange, ragged, long-haired tuft, called by woodsmen the "bell." His chest was of great depth, telling of exhaustless lung power; and his long forelegs upbore his mighty fore-shoulders so that their gaunt ridge was nearly seven feet from the ground. From this height his short back fell away on a slope to hindquarters disproportionately scant, so that had his appearance been altogether less imposing and formidable, he might have looked grotesque from some points of view. In the moonlight, of course, his colour was just a cold gray; but in the daytime it would have shown a rusty brown, paling and yellowing slightly on the under parts and inside the legs.

Having sniffed the air for several minutes without discerning anything to interest him, the great bull bethought him of his evening meal. With a sudden blowing out of his breath, he heaved his bulk about and made for the waterside, crashing down the bushes and making, in sheer wantonness, a noise that seemed out of keeping with the time and place. Several times he paused to thrash amid the undergrowth with his antlers. Reaching the water, he plunged in, thigh-deep, with great splashings, and sent the startled waves chasing each other in bright curves to the farther shore. There he stood and began pulling recklessly at the leaves and shoots of the water-lilies. He was hungry, indeed, yet his mind was little engrossed with his feeding.

As a rule, the moose, for all his bulk and seeming clumsiness, moves through the forest as soundlessly as a weasel. He plants his wide hoofs like thistle-down, insinuates his spread of antlers through the tangle like a snake, and befools his enemies with the nicest craft of the wilderness.

But this was the rutting season. The great bull was looking for his mate. He had a wild suspicion that the rest of the world was conspiring to keep him from her, and therefore he felt a fierce indignation against the rest of the world. He was ready to imagine a rival behind every bush. He wanted to find these rivals and fight them to the death. His blood was in an insurrection of madness, and suspense, and sweetness, and desire. He cared no more for craft, for concealment. He wanted all the forest to know just where he was — that his mate might come to be loved, that his rivals might come to be ground beneath his antlers and his hoofs. Therefore he went wildly, making all the noise he could; while the rest of the forest folk, unseen and withdrawn, looked on with disapproval and with expectation of the worst.

As he stood in the cool water, pulling and munching the lilies, there came a sound that stiffened him to instant movelessness. Up went his head, the streams trickling from it silverly; and he listened with every nerve of his body. It was a deeply sonorous, booming call, with a harsh catch in it, but softened to music by the distance. It came from some miles down the opposite shore of the lake. To the great bull's ears it was the sweetest music he could dream of — the only music, in fact, that interested him. It was the voice of his mate, calling him to the trysting-place.

He gave answer at once to the summons, contracting his flanks violently as he propelled the sound from his deep lungs. To one listening far down the lake the call would have sounded beautiful in its way, though lugubrious — a wild, vast, incomprehensible voice, appropriate to the solitude. But to a near-by listener it must have sounded both monstrous and absurd — like nothing else so much as the effort of a young farmyard bull to mimic the braying of an ass. Nevertheless, to one who could hear aright, it was a noble and splendid call, vital with all sincerity of response and love and elemental passion.

Having sent forth his reply, he waited for no more. He was consumed with fierce anxiety lest some rival should also hear and answer the invitation. Dashing forward into the deep water, he swam at great speed straight across the cove, leaving a wide wake behind him. The summons came again, but he could not reply while he was swimming. As soon as he reached land he answered, and

"HE GAVE ANSWER AT ONCE TO THE SUMMONS."

then started in mad haste down the shore, taking advantage of the open beach where there was any, but for the most part hidden in the trees, where his progress was loudly marked by the crashing and trampling of his impatience.

All the furtive kindred, great as well as small, bold as well as timorous, gave him wide berth. A huge black bear, pleasantly engaged in ripping open an ant stump right in his path, stepped aside into the gloom with a supercilious deferring. Farther down the lake a panther lay out along a maple limb, and watched the ecstatic moose rush by beneath. He dug his claws deeper into the bark, and bared his fangs thirstily; but he had no wish to attempt the perilous enterprise of stopping the moose on his love errand. From time to time, from that same enchanted spot down the lake, came the summons, growing reassuringly nearer; and from time to time the journeying bull would pause in his stride to give answer. Little flecks of foam blew from his nostrils, and his flanks were heaving, but his heart was joyous, and his eyes bright with anticipation.

Meanwhile, what was it that awaited him, in that enchanted spot by the waterside under the full moon, on which the eyes of his eager imagination were fixed so passionately as he crashed his wild way through the night? There was the little open of firm gravelly beach, such as all his tribe affected as their favoured place of trysting. But no brown young cow cast her shadow on the white gravel, standing with forefeet wide apart and neck outstretched to utter her desirous call. The beach lay bright and empty. Just back of it stood a spreading maple, its trunk veiled in a thicket of viburnum and withe-wood. Back of this again a breadth of lighted open, carrying no growth but low kalmia scrub. It was a highly satisfactory spot for the hunter who follows his sport in the calling season.

There was no brown young cow anywhere within hearing; but in the covert of the viburnum, under the densest shadow of the maple, crouched two hunters, their eyes peering through the leafage with the keen glitter of those of a beast of prey in ambush. One of these hunters was a mere boy, clad in blue-gray homespuns, lank and sprawling of limb, the whitish down just beginning to acquire texture and definiteness on his ruddy but hawk-like face. He was on his first moose-hunt, eager for a trophy, and ambitious to learn moose-calling. The other was a raw-boned and grizzled woodsman, still-eyed, swarthy-faced, and affecting the Indian

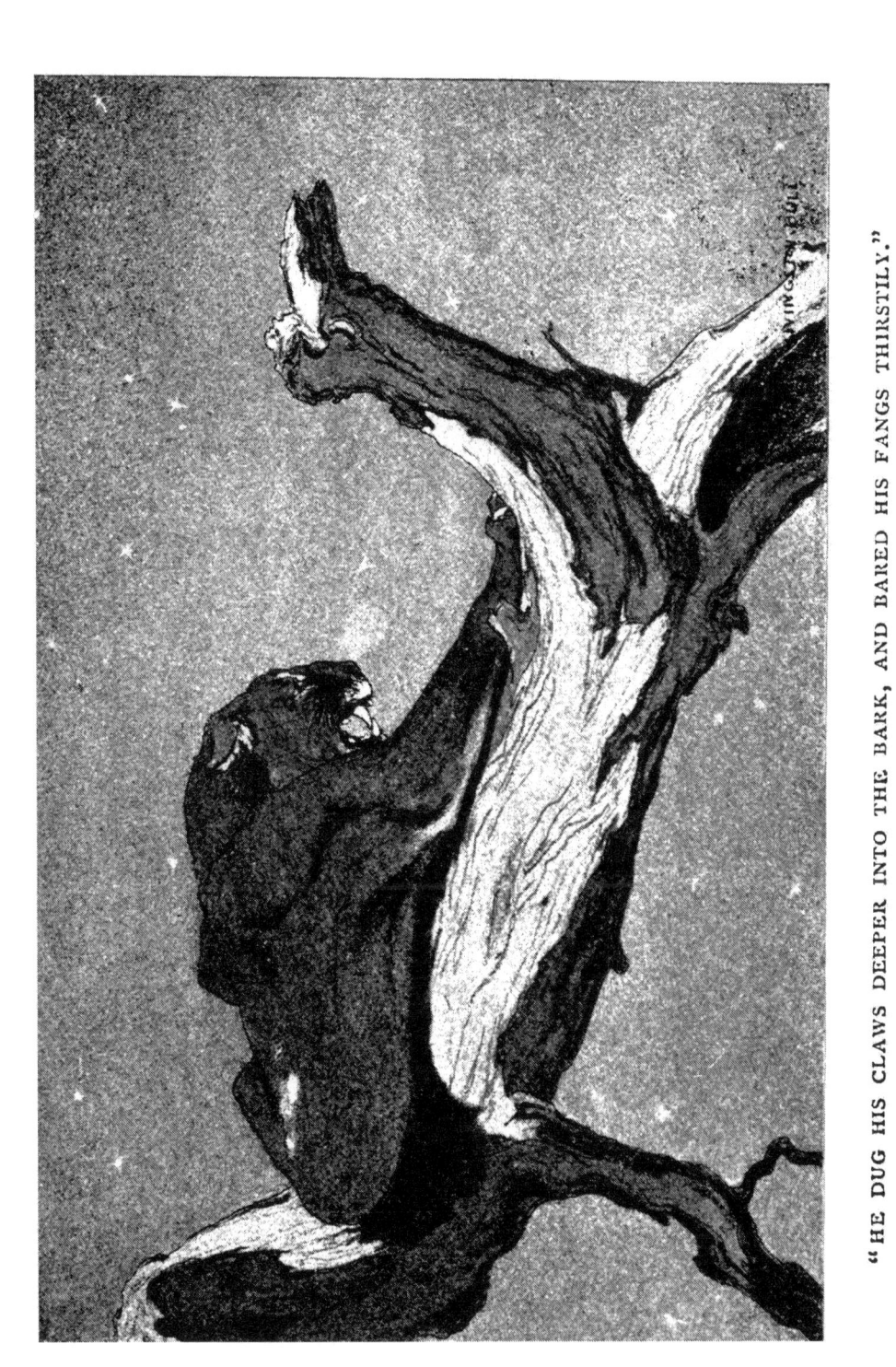

"HE DUG HIS CLAWS DEEPER INTO THE BARK, AND BARED HIS FANGS THIRSTILY."

fashion of a buckskin jacket. He was a hunter whose fame went wide in the settlement. He could master and slay the cunning kindred of the wild by a craft finer than their own. He knew all their weaknesses, and played upon them to their destruction as he would. In one hairy hand he held a long, trumpet-like roll of birch-bark. This he would set to his lips at intervals, and utter through it his deadly perfect mimicry of the call of the cow-moose in rutting season. Each time he did so, there came straightway in response the ever-nearing bellow of the great bull hurrying exultantly to the tryst. Each time he did so, too, the boy crouching beside him turned upon him a look of marvelling awe, the look of the rapt neophyte. This tribute the old woodsman took as his bare due, and paid it no attention whatever.

While yet the approaching bull was apparently so far off that even eyes so keen as his had no chance of discovering the ambush, the younger hunter, unused to so long a stillness, got up to stretch his cramped legs. As he stood forth into the moonlight, a loon far out in the silver sheen of the lake descried him, and at once broke into a peal of his startling and demoniacal laughter.

"Git down!" ordered the old woodsman, curtly.

"That bird tells all it sees!" And immediately setting the birchen trumpet to his lips, he sounded the most seductive call he knew. It was answered promptly, and this time from so near at hand that the nerves of both hunters were strung to instant tension. They both effaced themselves to a stillness and invisibility not excelled by that of the most secret of the furtive folk. In this stillness the boy, who was himself, by nature and affinity, of the woodland kin, caught for the first time that subtle, rhythmic hr-r-r-r-r-ing of the forest pulse; but he took it for merely the rushing of the blood in his too attentive ears.

Presently this sound was forgotten. He heard a great portentous crashing in the underbrush. Nearer, nearer it came; and both men drew themselves together, as if to meet a shock. Their eyes met for one instant, and the look spoke astonished realisation of the giant approaching bulk. Then the old hunter called once more. The answer, resonant and vast, but almost shrill with the ecstasy of passion, blared forth from a dense fir thicket immediately beyond the moonlit open. The mighty crashing came up, as it seemed, to the very edge of the glade, and there stopped abruptly. No towering flight of antlers emerged into the light.

A Treason of Nature

The boy's rifle — for it was his shot — was at his shoulder; but he lowered it, and anxiously his eyes sought the face of his companion. The latter, with lips that made no sound, shaped the words, "He suspects something." Then, once more lifting the treacherous tube of birch-bark to his mouth, he murmured through it a rough but strangely tender note. It was not utterly unlike that with which a cow sometimes speaks to her calf just after giving birth to it, but more nasal and vibrant; and it was full of caressing expectancy, and desire, and question, and half-reproach. All the yearning of all the mating ardour that has triumphed over insatiable death, and kept the wilderness peopled from the first, was in that deceitful voice. As he ceased the call he raised himself stealthily behind the thick trunk of the maple, lifted a wooden bucket of water to the height of his shoulder, and poured out a stream, which fell with noisy splashing on the gravel.

The eager moose could not resist the appeal. His vague suspicions fled. He burst forth into the open, his eyes full and bright, his giant head proudly uplifted.

The boy's large-calibre rifle spoke at that instant, with a bitter, clapping report, and a shoot of red flame through the viburnum screen. The tall moose neither saw nor heard it. The leaden death had crashed through his brain even before his quick sense had time to note the menace. Swerving a little at the shock, the huge body sank forward upon the knees and muzzle, then rolled over upon its side. There he lay unstirring, betrayed by nature in the hour of his anticipation.

With a sudden outburst of voices, the two hunters sprang up, broke from their ambush, and ran to view the prize. They were no longer of the secretive kindred of the wilderness, but pleased children. The old woodsman eyed shrewdly the inimitable spread of the prostrate antlers. As for the boy, he stared at his victim, breathless, his eyes a-glitter with the fierce elemental pride of the hunter triumphant.

THE HAUNTER
OF THE
PINE GLOOMS

The Haunter of the Pine Gloom

FOR a moment the Boy felt afraid — afraid in his own woods. He felt that he was being followed, that there were hostile eyes burning into the back of his jacket. The sensation was novel to him, as well as unpleasant, and he resented it. He knew it was all nonsense. There was nothing in these woods bigger than a weasel, he was sure of that. Angry at himself, he would not look round, but swung along carelessly through the thicket, being in haste because it was already late and the cows should have been home and milked before sundown. Suddenly, however, he remembered that it was going flat against all woodcraft to disregard a warning. And was he not, indeed, deliberately seeking to cultivate and sharpen his instincts, in the effort to get closer to the wild woods folk and know them in their furtive lives? Moreover, he was certainly getting more and more afraid! He stopped, and peered into the pine glooms which surrounded him.

Standing motionless as a stump, and breathing with perfect soundlessness, he strained his ears to help his eyes in their questioning of this obscure menace. He could see nothing. He could hear nothing. Yet he knew his eyes and ears were cunning to pierce all the wilderness disguises. But stay — was that a deeper shadow, merely, far among the pine trunks? And — did it move? He stole forward; but even as he did so, whatever of unusual he saw or fancied in the object upon which his eyes were fixed, melted away. It became but a shadow among other shadows, and motionless as they — all motionless in the calm of the tranquil sunset. He ran forward now, impatient to satisfy himself beyond suspicion. Yes — of course — it was just this gray spruce stump! He turned away, a little puzzled and annoyed in spite of himself. Thrashing noisily hither and thither through the underbrush, — quite contrary to his wonted quietude while in the domains of the wood folk, — and calling loudly in his clear young voice, "Co-petty! Co-petty! Co-petty! Co-o-o-petty!" over and over, he at length found the wilful young cow which had been eluding him. Then he drove the herd slowly homeward, with mellow *tink-a-tonk, tank-tonk* of the cow-bells, to the farmyard and the milking.

Several evenings later, when his search for the wilful young cow chanced to lead him again through the corner of this second growth pine wood, the Boy had a repetition of the disturbing experience. This time his response was instant and aggressive. As soon as he felt that sensation of unfriendly eyes pursuing him, he turned, swept the shadows with his piercing scrutiny, plunged into the thickets with a rush, then stopped short as if frozen, almost holding his breath in the tensity of his stillness. By this procedure he hoped to catch the unknown haunter of the glooms under the disadvantage of motion. But again he was baffled. Neither eye nor ear revealed him anything. He went home troubled and wondering.

Some evenings afterward the same thing happened at another corner of the pasture; and again one morning when he was fishing in the brook a mile back into the woods, where it ran through a tangled growth of birch and fir. He began to feel that he was either the object of a malicious scrutiny, or that he was going back to those baby days when he used to be afraid of the dark. Being just at the age of ripe boyhood when childishness in himself would seem least endurable, the latter supposition was not to be considered. He therefore set himself to investigate the mystery, and to pit his woodcraft against the evasiveness of this troubler of his peace.

The Boy's confidence in his woodcraft was well founded. His natural aptitude for the study of the wild kindred had been cultivated to the utmost of his opportunity, in all the time that could be stolen from his lesson-hours and from his unexacting duties about his father's place. Impatient and boyish in other matters, he had trained himself to the patience of an Indian in regard to all matters appertaining to the wood folk. He had a pet theory that the human animal was more competent, as a mere animal, than it gets the credit of being; and it was his particular pride to outdo the wild creatures at their own games. He could hide, unstirring as a hidden grouse. He could run down a deer by sheer endurance — only to spare it at the last and let it go, observed and mastered, but unhurt. And he could see, as few indeed among the wild things could. This was his peculiar triumph. His eyes could discriminate where theirs could not. Perfect movelessness was apt to deceive the keenest of them; but his sight was not to be so foiled. He could differentiate gradually the shape of the brown hare crouching motionless on its brown

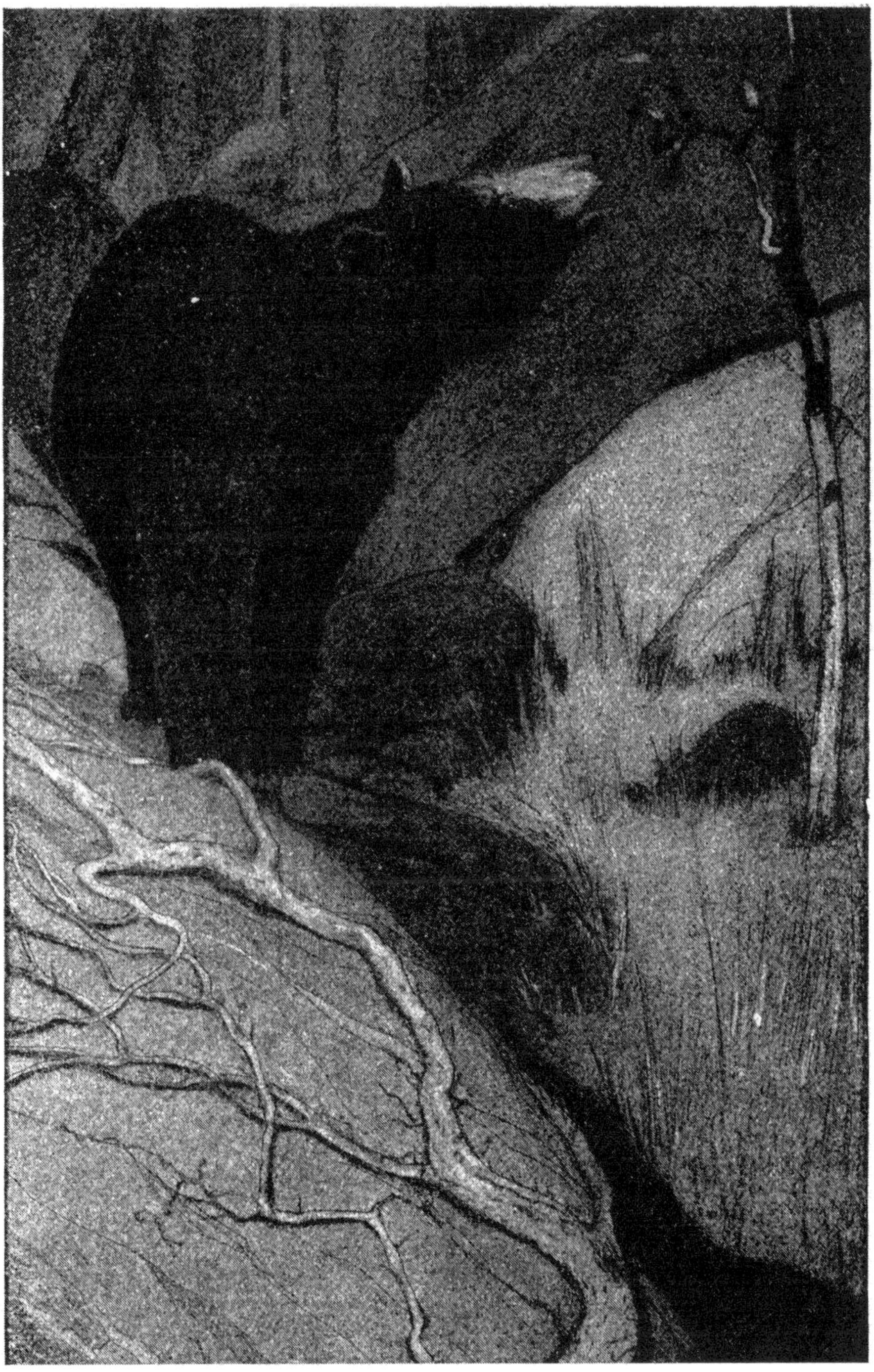

form; and separate the yellow weasel from the tuft of yellow weeds; and distinguish the slumbering night-hawk from the knot on the hemlock limb. He could hear, too, as well as most of the wild kindred, and better, indeed, than some; but in this he had to acknowledge himself hopelessly outclassed by not a few. He knew that the wood-mouse and the hare, for instance, would simply make a mock of him in any test of ears; and as for the owl — well, that gifted hearer of infinitesimal sounds would be justified in calling him stone-deaf.

The Boy was a good shot, but very seldom was it that he cared to display his skill in that direction. It was his ambition to "name all the birds without a gun." He would know the wild folk living, not dead. From the feebler of the wild folk he wanted trust, not fear; and he himself had no fear, on the other hand, of the undisputed Master of the Woods, the big black bear. His faith, justified by experience, was that the bear had sense, knew how to mind his own business, and was ready to let other people mind theirs. He knew the bear well, from patient, secret observation when the big beast little imagined himself observed. From the neighbourhood of a bull-moose in rutting season he would have taken pains to absent himself; and if he had ever come across any trace of a panther in those regions, he would have studied that uncertain beast with his rifle always at hand in case of need. For the rest, he felt safe in the woods, as an initiate of their secrets, and it was unusual for him to carry in his wanderings any weapon but a stout stick and the sheath-knife in his belt.

Now, however, when he set himself to discover what it was that haunted his footsteps in the gloom, he took his little rifle — and in this act betrayed to himself more uneasiness than he had been willing to acknowledge.

This especial afternoon he got the hired man to look after the cows for him, and betook himself early, about two hours before sundown, to the young pine wood where the mystery had begun. In the heart of a little thicket, where he was partly concealed and where the gray-brown of his clothes blended with the stems and dead branches, he seated himself comfortably with his back against a stump. Experience had taught him that, in order to hold himself long in one position, the position chosen must be an easy one. Soon his muscles relaxed, and all his senses rested, watchful but unstrained. He had learned that tensity was a thing to be held in reserve until occasion should call for it.

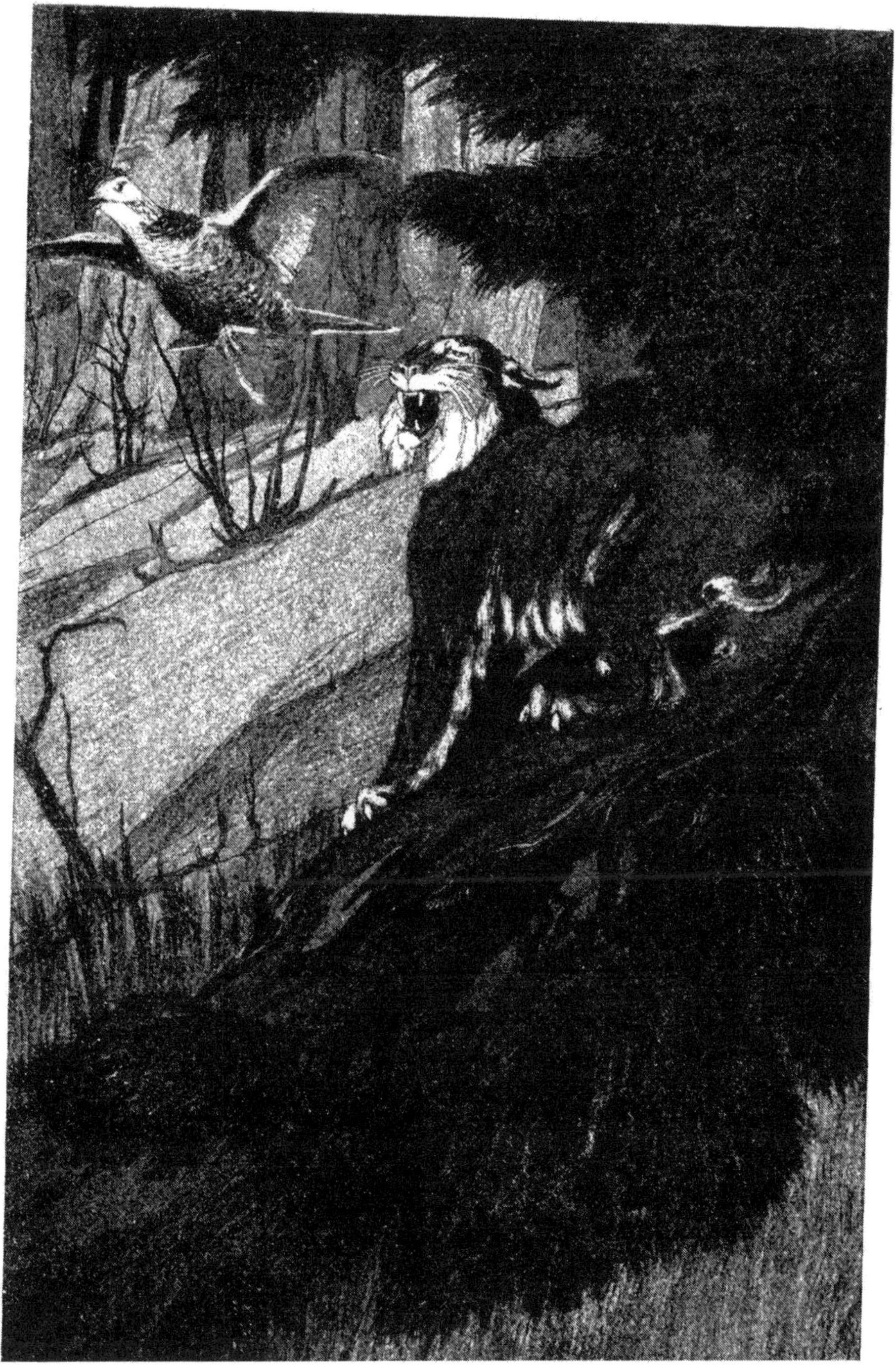

In a little while his presence was ignored or forgotten by the chipmunks, the chickadees, the whitethroats, and other unafraid creatures. Once a chipmunk, on weighty business bent, ran over his legs rather than go around so unoffending an obstacle. The chickadees played antics on the branches, and the air was beaded sweetly everywhere with their familiar *sic-a-dee, dee-ee.* A white-throat in the tree right over his head whistled his mellow *dear, dear eedledee—eedledee—eedledee,* over and over. But there was nothing new in all this: and at length he began to grow conscious of his position, and desirous of changing it slightly.

Before he had quite made up his mind to this momentous step there came upon his ear a beating of wings, and a fine cock grouse alighted on a log some forty paces distant. He stretched himself, strutted, spread his ruff and wings and tail, and was about to begin drumming. But before the first sonorous note rolled out there was a rustle and a pounce. The beautiful bird bounded into the air as if hurled from a spring; and a great lynx landed on the log, digging his claws fiercely into the spot where the grouse had stood. As the bird rocketed off through the trees the lynx glared after him, and emitted a loud, screeching snarl of rage. His disappointment was so obvious and childish that the Boy almost laughed out.

"Lucifee," said he to himself, giving it the name it went by in all the back settlements. "That's the fellow that has been haunting me. I didn't think there were any lynxes this side of the mountain. He hasn't seen me, that's sure. So now it's my turn to haunt him a bit."

The lucifee, indeed, had for the moment thrown off all concealment, in his fury at the grouse's escape. His stub of a tail twitched and his pale bright eyes looked around for something on which to vent his feelings. Suddenly, however, a wandering puff of air blew the scent of the Boy to his nostrils. On the instant, like the soundless melting of a shadow, he was down behind the log, taking observations through the veil of a leafy branch.

Though the animal was looking straight toward him, the Boy felt sure he was not seen. The eyes, indeed, were but following the nose. The lynx's nose is not so keen and accurate in its information as are the noses of most of the other wild folk, and the animal was puzzled. The scent was very familiar to him, for had he not been investigating the owner of it for over a week, following him at every opportunity with mingled curiosity and hatred? Now, judging by the scent, the object of his curiosity was close at hand — yet incomprehensibly invisible. After sniffing and peering for some minutes he came out from behind the log and crept forward, moving like a shadow, and following up the scent. From bush to tree-trunk, from thicket to stump, he glided with incredible smoothness and rapidity, elusive to the eye, utterly inaudible; and behind each shelter he crouched to again take observations. The Boy thought of him, now, as a sort of malevolent ghost in fur, and no longer wondered that he had failed to catch a glimpse of him before.

The lynx (this was the first of its tribe the Boy had ever seen, but he knew the kind by reputation) was a somewhat doggish-looking cat, perhaps four or five times the weight of an ordinary Tom, and with a very uncatlike length of leg in proportion to its length of body. Its hindquarters were disproportionately high, its tail ridiculously short. Spiky tufts to its ears and a peculiar brushing back of the fur beneath its chin gave its round and fierce-eyed countenance an expression at once savage and grotesque. Most grotesque of all were the huge, noiseless pads of its feet, muffled in fur. Its colour was a tawny, weather-beaten gray-brown; its eyes pale, round, brilliant, and coldly cruel.

At length the animal, on a stronger puff of air, located the scent more closely. This was obvious from a sudden stiffening of his muscles. His eyes began to discern a peculiarity in the pine trunk some twenty paces ahead. Surely that was no ordinary pine trunk, that! No, indeed, that was where the scent of the Boy came from — and the hair on his back bristled fiercely. In fact, it *was* the Boy! The lucifee's first impulse, on the discovery, was to shrink off like a mist, and leave further investigation to a more favourable opportunity. But he thought better of it because the Boy was so still. Could he be asleep? Or, perhaps, dead? At any rate, it would seem, he was for the moment harmless. Curiosity overcoming discretion, and possibly hatred suggesting a chance of advantageous attack, the animal lay down, his paws folded under him, contemplatively, and studied with round, fierce eyes the passive figure beneath the tree.

The Boy, meanwhile, returned the stare with like interest, but through narrowed lids, lest his eyes should betray him; and his heart beat fast with the excitement of the situation. There was a most thrilling uncertainty, indeed, as to what the animal would do next. He was glad he had brought his rifle.

"PRESENTLY THE LUCIFEE AROSE AND BEGAN CREEPING

Presently the lucifee arose and began creeping stealthily closer, at the same time swerving off to the right as if to get behind the tree. Whether his purpose in this was to escape unseen or to attack from the rear, the Boy could not decide; but what he did decide was that the game was becoming hazardous and should be brought to immediate close. He did not want to be compelled to shoot the beast in self-defence, for, this being the first lynx he had ever seen, he wanted to study him. So, suddenly, with the least possible movement of his features, he squeaked like a wood-mouse, then *quit-quit*-ed like a grouse, then gave to a nicety the sonorous call of the great horned owl.

The astonished lynx seemed to shrink into himself, as he flattened against the ground, grown moveless as a stone. It was incredible, appalling indeed, that these familiar and well-understood voices should all come from that same impassive figure. He crouched unstirring for so long that at last the shadows began to deepen perceptibly. The Boy remembered that he had heard, some time ago, the bells of the returning cows; and he realised that it might not be well to give his adversary the advantage of the dark. Nevertheless, the experience was one of absorbing interest and he hated to close it.

At length the lucifee came to the conclusion that the mystery should be probed more fully. Once more he rose upon his padded, soundless paws, and edged around stealthily to get behind the tree. This was not to be permitted. The Boy burst into a peal of laughter and rose slowly to his feet. On the instant the lucifee gave a bound, like a great rubber ball, backward into a thicket. It seemed as if his big feet were all feathers, and as if every tree trunk bent to intervene and screen his going. The Boy rubbed his eyes, bewildered at so complete and instantaneous an exit. Grasping his rifle in readiness, he hurried forward, searching every thicket, looking behind every stump and trunk. The haunter of the gloom had disappeared.

After this, however, the Boy was no more troubled by the mysterious pursuit. The lynx had evidently found out all he required to know about him. On the other hand the Boy was balked in his purpose of finding out all he wanted to know about the lynx. That wary animal eluded all his most patient and ingenious lyings-in-wait, until the Boy began to feel that his woodcraft was being turned to a derision. Only once more that autumn did he catch a glimpse of his shy opponent, and then by chance, when he was on another trail. Hidden

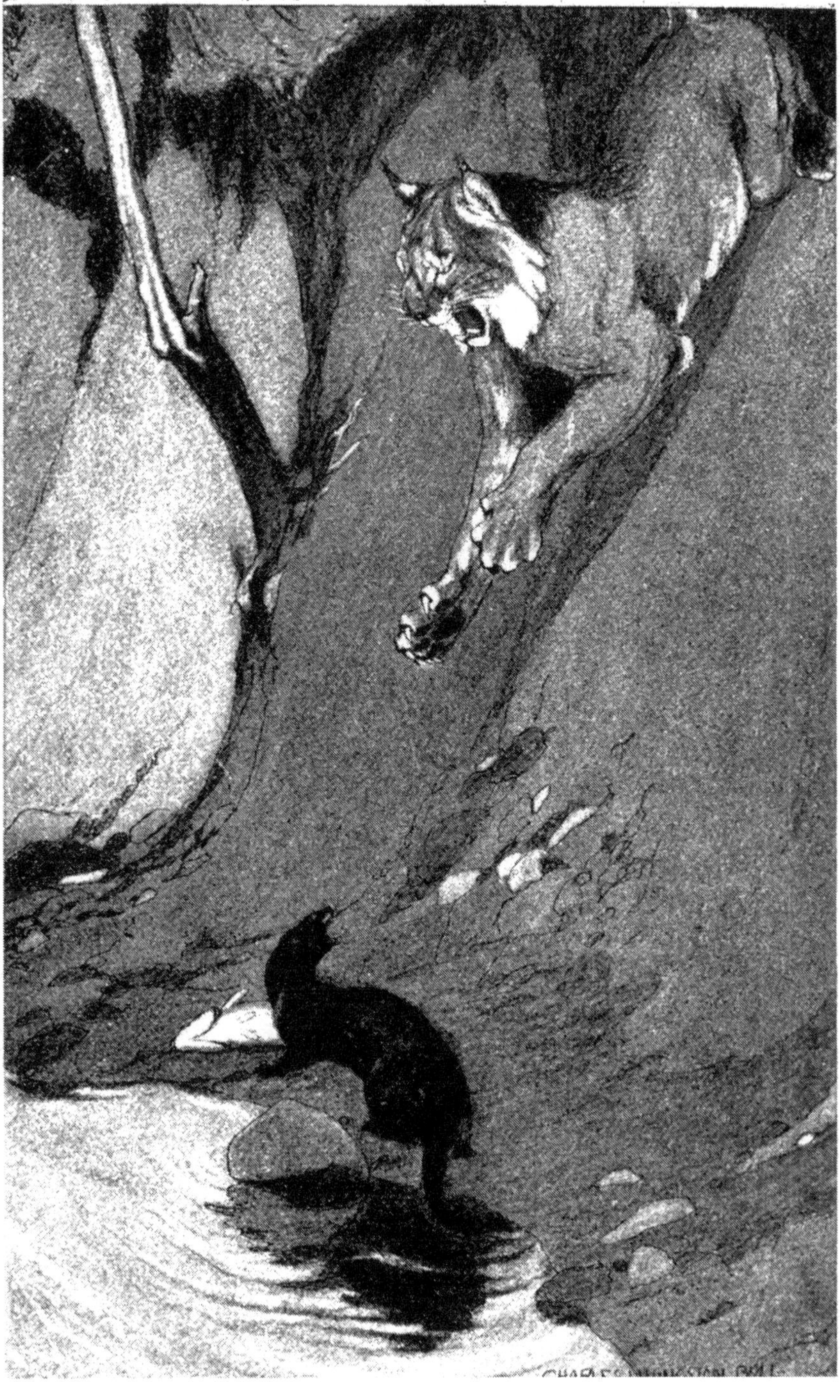

The Haunter of the Pine Gloom

at the top of a thick-wooded bank he was watching a mink at its fishing in the brook below. But as it turned out, the dark little fisherman had another watcher as well. The pool in the brook was full of large suckers. The mink had just brought one to land in his triangular jaws and was proceeding to devour it, when a silent gray thunderbolt fell upon him. There was a squeak and a snarl; and the long, snaky body of the mink lay as still as that of the fish which had been its prey. Crouching over his double booty, a paw on each, the lynx glared about him in exultant pride. The scent of the Boy, high on the bank above, did not come to him. The fish, as the more highly prized tidbit, he devoured at once. Then, after licking his lips and polishing his whiskers, he went loping off through the woods with the limp body of the mink hanging from his jaws, to eat it at leisure in his lair. The Boy made up his mind to find out where that lair was hidden. But his searchings were all vain, and he tried to console himself with the theory that the animal was wont to travel great distances in his hunting — a theory which he knew in his heart to be contrary to the customs of the cat-kindred.

During the winter he was continually tantalised

by coming across the lucifee's tracks — great footprints, big enough to do for the trail-signature of the panther himself. If he followed these tracks far he was sure to find interesting records of wilderness adventure — here a spot where the lynx had sprung upon a grouse, and missed it, or upon a hare, and caught it; and once he found the place where the big furry paws had dug down to the secret white retreat where a grouse lay sleeping under the snow. But by and by the tracks would cross each other, and make wide circles, or end in a tree where there was no lucifee to be found. And the Boy was too busy at home to give the time which he saw it would require to unravel the maze to its end. But he refused to consider himself defeated. He merely regarded his triumph as postponed.

Early in the spring the triumph came — though not just the triumph he had expected. Before the snow was quite gone, and when the sap was beginning to flow from the sugar maples, he went with the hired man to tap a grove of extra fine trees some five miles east from the settlement. Among the trees they had a sugar camp; and when not at the sugar-making, the Boy explored a near-by burnt-land ridge, very rocky and rich in coverts, where he had often thought the old lynx, his adversary, might have made his lair. Here, the second day after his arrival, he came upon a lucifee track. But it was not the track with which he was familiar. It was smaller, and the print of the right forefoot lacked a toe.

The Boy grinned happily and rubbed his mittened hands. "Aha!" said he to himself, "better and better! There is a Mrs. Lucifee. Now we'll see where she hides her kittens."

The trail was an easy one this time, for no enemies had been looked for in that desert neighbourhood. He followed it for about half a mile, and then caught sight of a hollow under an overhanging rock, to which the tracks seemed to lead. Working around to get the wind in his face, he stole cautiously nearer, till he saw that the hollow was indeed the entrance to a cave, and that the tracks led directly into it. He had no desire to investigate further, with the risk of finding the lucifee at home; and it was getting too late for him to undertake his usual watching tactics. He withdrew stealthily and returned to the camp in exultation.

In the night a thaw set in, so the Boy was spared the necessity of waiting for the noon sun to soften the snow and make the walking noiseless. He set out on the very edge of sunrise, and reached his hiding-place while the mouth of the cave was still in shadow. On the usual crisp mornings of sugar season the snow at such an hour would have borne a crust, to crackle sharply under every footstep and proclaim an intruding presence to all the wood folk for a quarter of a mile about.

After waiting for a good half-hour, his eyes glued to a small black opening under the rock, his heart gave a leap of strong, joyous excitement. He saw the lucifee's head appear in the doorway. She peered about her cautiously, little dreaming, however, that there was any cause for caution. Then she came forth into the blue morning light, yawned hugely, and stretched herself like a cat. She was smaller than the Boy's old adversary, somewhat browner in hue, leaner, and of a peculiarly malignant expression. The Boy had an instant intuition that she would be the more dangerous antagonist of the two; and a feeling of sharp hostility toward her, such as he had never felt toward her mate, arose in his heart.

When she had stretched to her satisfaction, and washed her face perfunctorily with two or three sweeps of her big paw, she went back into the cave. In two or three minutes she reappeared, and this

CHARLES
LIVINGSTON BULL.

time with a brisk air of purpose. She turned to the right, along a well-worn trail, ran up a tree to take a survey of the country, descended hastily, and glided away among the thickets.

"It's breakfast she's after," said the Boy to himself, "and she'll take some time to find it."

When she had been some ten minutes gone, the Boy went boldly down to the cave. He had no fear of encountering the male, because he knew from an old hunter who had taught him his first wood-lore that the male lucifee is not popular with his mate at whelping time, having a truly Saturnian fashion of devouring his own offspring. But there was the possibility, remote, indeed, but disquieting, of the mother turning back to see to some neglected duty; and with this chance in view he held his rifle ready.

Inside the cave he stood still and waited for his eyes to get used to the gloom. Then he discovered, in one corner, on a nest of fur and dry grass, a litter of five lucifee whelps. They were evidently very young, little larger than ordinary kittens, and too young to know fear, but their eyes were wide open, and they stood up on strong legs when he touched them softly with his palm. Disappointed in their expectation of being nursed, they mewed, and there was something in their cries that sounded strangely wild and fierce. To the Boy's great surprise, they were quite different in colour from their gray-brown, unmarked parents, being striped vividly and profusely, like a tabby or tiger. The Boy was delighted with them, and made up his mind that when they were a few days older he would take two of them home with him to be brought up in the ways of civilisation.

Three days later he again visited the den, this time with a basket in which to carry away his prizes. After waiting an hour to see if the mother were anywhere about, he grew impatient. Stealing as close to the cave's mouth as the covert would permit, he squeaked like a wood-mouse several times. This seductive sound bringing no response, he concluded that the old lucifee must be absent. He went up to the mouth of the cave and peered in, holding his rifle in front of his face in readiness for an instant shot. When his eyes got command of the dusk, he saw to his surprise that the den was empty. He entered and felt the vacant nest. It was quite cold, and had a deserted air. Then he realised what had happened, and cursed his clumsiness. The old lucifee, when she came back to her den, had learned by means of her nose that her enemy had discovered her hiding-place and touched her young with his defiling human hands, thereupon in wrath she had carried them away to some remote and unviolated lair. Till they were grown to nearly the full stature of lucifee destructiveness, the Boy saw no more of his wonderful lucifee kittens.

Toward the latter part of the summer, however, he began to think that perhaps he had made a mistake in leaving these fierce beasts to multiply. He no longer succeeded in catching sight of them as they went about their furtive business, for they had somehow become aware of his woodcraft and distrustful of their own shifts. But on all sides he found trace of their depredations among the weaker creatures. He observed that the rabbits were growing scarce about the settlement; and even the grouse were less numerous in the upland thickets of young birch. As all the harmless wood folk were his friends, he began to feel that he had been false to them in sparing their enemies. Thereupon, he took to carrying his rifle whenever he went exploring. He had not really declared war upon the haunters of the glooms, but his relations with them were becoming distinctly strained.

At length the rupture came; and it was violent.

In one of the upland pastures, far back from the settlement, he came upon the torn carcass of a half-grown lamb. He knew that this was no work of a bear, for the berries were abundant that autumn, and the bear prefers berries to mutton. Moreover, when a bear kills a sheep he skins it deftly and has the politeness to leave the pelt rolled up in a neat bundle, just to indicate to the farmer that he has been robbed by a gentleman. But this carcass was torn and mangled most untidily; and the Boy divined the culprits.

It was early in the afternoon when he made his find, and he concluded that the lucifees were likely to return to their prey before evening. He hid himself, therefore, behind a log thickly fringed with juniper, not twenty-five paces from the carcass; and waited, rifle in hand.

A little before sunset appeared the five young lucifees, now nearly full grown. They fell at once to tearing at the carcass, with much jealous snarling and fighting. Soon afterwards came the mother, with a well-fed, leisurely air; and at her heels, the big male of the Boy's first acquaintance. It was evident that, now that the rabbits were getting scarce, the lucifees were hunting in packs, a custom very unusual with these unsocial beasts under ordi-

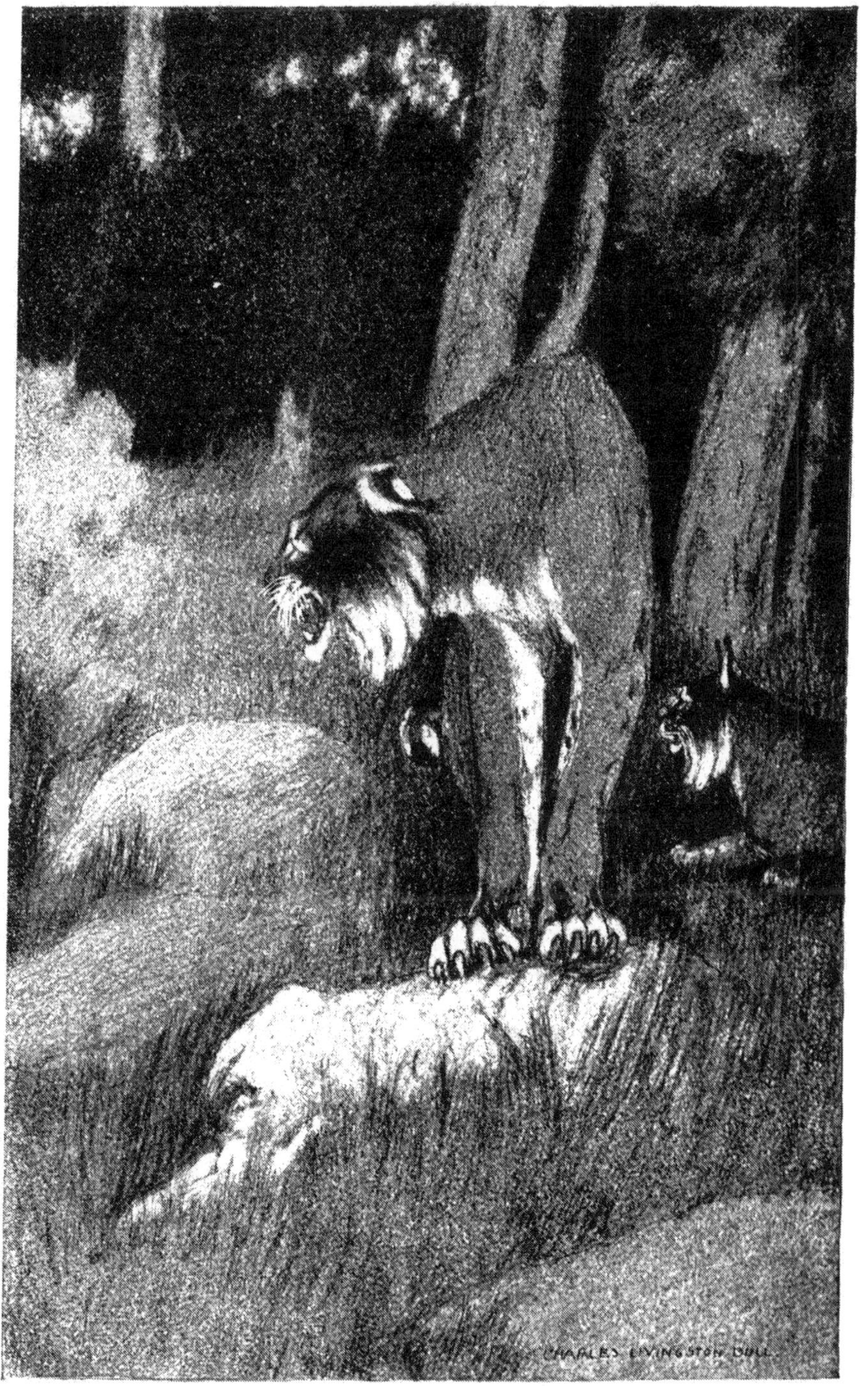
CHARLES LIVINGSTON BULL

nary circumstances, and only adopted when seeking big game. The big male cuffed the cubs aside without ceremony, mounted the carcass with an air of lordship, glared about him, and suddenly, with a snarl of wrath, fixed his eyes upon the green branches wherein the Boy lay concealed. At the same time the female, who had stopped short, sniffing and peering suspiciously, crouched to her belly, and began to crawl very softly and stealthily, as a cat crawls upon an unsuspecting bird, toward the innocent-looking juniper thicket.

The Boy realised that he had presumed too far upon the efficacy of stillness, and that the lynxes, at this close range, had detected him. He realised, too, that now, jealous in the possession of their prey, they had somehow laid aside their wonted fear of him; and he congratulated himself heartily that his little rifle was a repeater. Softly he raised it to take aim at the nearest, and to him the most dangerous of his foes, the cruel-eyed female; but in doing so he stirred, ever so little, the veiling fringe of juniper. At the motion the big male sprang forward, with two great bounds, and crouched within ten yards of the log. His stub of a tail twitched savagely. He was plainly nerving himself to the attack.

There was no time to lose. Taking quick but careful aim, the Boy fired. The bullet found its mark between the brute's eyes, and he straightened out where he lay, without a kick. At the sound and the flash the female doubled upon herself as quick as light; and before the Boy could get a shot at her she was behind a stump some rods away, shrinking small, and fleeing like a gray shred of vapour. The whelps, too, had vanished with almost equal skill — all but one. He, less alert and intelligent than his fellows, tried concealment behind a clump of pink fireweed. But the Boy's eyes pierced the screen; and the next bullet, cutting the fireweed stalks, took vengeance for many slaughtered hares and grouse.

After this the Boy saw no more of his enemies for some months, but though they had grown still more wary their experience had not made them less audacious. Before the snow fell they had killed another sheep; and the Boy was sure that they, rather than any skunks or foxes, were to blame for the disappearance of several geese from his flock. His primeval hunting instincts were now aroused, and he was no longer merely the tender-hearted and sympathetic observer. It was only toward the marauding lucifees, however, that his feelings had changed. The rest of the wild folk he loved as well as before, but for the time he was too busy to think of them.

When the snow came, and footsteps left their telltale records, the Boy found to his surprise that he had but one lucifee to deal with. Every lynx track in the neighbourhood had a toe missing on the right forefoot. It was clear that the whelps of last spring had shirked the contest and betaken themselves to other and safer hunting-grounds; but he felt that between himself and the vindictive old female it was war to the knife. Her tracks fairly quartered the outlying fields all about his father's farm, and were even to be found now and again around the sheep-pen and the fowl-house. Yet never, devise he ever so cunningly, did he get a glimpse of so much as her gray stub tail.

At last, through an open window, she invaded the sheep-pen by night and killed two young ewes. To the Boy this seemed mere wantonness of cruelty, and he set his mind to a vengeance which he had hitherto been unwilling to consider. He resolved to trap his enemy, since he could not shoot her.

Now, as a mere matter of woodcraft, he knew all about trapping and snaring; but ever since the day, now five years gone, when he had been heart-stricken by his first success in rabbit-snaring, he had hated everything like a snare or trap. Now, however, in the interests of all the helpless creatures of the neighbourhood, wild or tame, he made up his mind to snare the lucifee. He went about it with his utmost skill, in a fashion taught him by an old Indian trapper.

Close beside one of his foe's remoter runways, in an upland field where the hares were still abundant, the Boy set his snare. It was just a greatly exaggerated rabbit snare, of extra heavy wire and a cord of triple strength. But instead of being attached to the top of a bent-down sapling, it was fastened to a billet of wood about four feet long and nearly two inches in diameter. This substantial stick was supported on two forked uprights driven into the snow beside the runway. Then young fir-bushes were stuck about it carefully in a way to conceal evidence of his handiwork; and an artful arrangement of twigs disguised the ambushed loop of wire.

Just behind the loop of wire, and some inches below it, the Boy arranged his bait. This consisted of the head and skin of a hare, stuffed carefully with straw, and posed in a lifelike attitude. It seemed, indeed, to be comfortably sleeping on the snow, under the branches of a young fir-tree; and the Boy felt confident that the tempting sight would prevent the wily old lucifee from taking any thought to the surroundings before securing the prize.

Late that afternoon, when rose and gold were in the sky, and the snowy open spaces were of a fainter rose, and the shadows took on an ashy purple under the edges of the pines and firs, the old lucifee came drifting along like a phantom. She peered hungrily under every bush, hoping to catch some careless hare asleep. On a sudden a greenish fire flamed into her wide eyes. She crouched, and moved even more stealthily than was her wont. The snow, the trees, the still, sweet evening light, seemed to invest her with silence. Very soundly it slept, that doomed hare, crouching under the fir-bush! And now, she was within reach of her spring. She shot forward, straight and strong and true.

Her great paws covered the prey, indeed; but at the same instant a sharp, firm grip clutched her throat with a jerk, and then something hit her a sharp rap over the shoulders. With a wild leap backward and aside she sought to evade the mysterious attack. But the noose settled firmly behind her ears, and the billet of wood, with a nasty tug at her throat, leapt after her.

So this paltry thing was her assailant! She flew into a wild rage at the stick, tearing at it with her teeth and claws. But this made no difference with the grip about her throat, so she backed off again. The stick followed — and the grip tightened. Bracing her forepaws upon the wood she pulled fiercely to free herself; and the wire drew taut till her throat was almost closed. Her rage had hastened her doom, fixing the noose where there was no such thing as clawing it off. Then fear took the place of rage in her savage heart. Her lungs seemed bursting. She began to realise that it was not the stick, but some more potent enemy whom she must circumvent or overcome. She picked up the billet between her jaws, climbed a big birch-tree which grew close by, ran out upon a limb some twenty feet from the ground, and dropped the stick, thinking thus to rid herself of the throttling burden.

The shock, as the billet reached the end of its drop, jerked her from her perch; but clutching frantically she gained a foothold on another limb eight or ten feet lower down. There she clung, her tongue out, her eyes filming, her breath stopped, strange colours of flame and darkness rioting in her brain. Bracing herself with all her remaining strength against the pull of the dangling stick, she got one paw firmly fixed against a small jutting branch. Thus it happened that when, a minute later, her life went out and she fell, she fell on the other side of the limb. The billet of wood flew up, caught in a fork, and held fast; and the limp, tawny body, twitching for a minute convulsively, hung some six or seven feet above its own tracks in the snow.

An hour or two later the moon rose, silvering the open spaces. Then, one by one and two by two, the hares came leaping down the aisles of pine and fir. Hither and thither around the great birch-tree they played, every now and then stopping to sit up and thump challenges to their rivals. And because it was quite still, they never saw the body of their deadliest foe, hanging stark from the branch above them.

THE WATCHERS OF THE CAMP FIRE

The Watchers of the Camp=Fire

FOR five years the big panther, who ruled the ragged plateau around the head waters of the Upsalquitch, had been well content with his hunting-ground. This winter, however, it had failed him. His tawny sides were lank with hunger. Rabbits — and none too many of them — were but thin and spiritless meat for such fiery blood as his. His mighty and restless muscles consumed too swiftly the unsatisfying food; and he was compelled to hunt continually, foregoing the long, recuperative sleeps which the tense springs of his organism required. Every fibre in his body was hungering for a full meal of red-blooded meat, the sustaining flesh of deer or caribou. The deer, of course, he did not expect on these high plains and rough hills of the Upsalquitch. They loved the well-wooded ridges of the sheltered, low-lying lands. But the caribou — for five years their wandering herds had thronged these plains, where the mosses they loved grew luxuriantly. And now, without warning or excuse, they had vanished.

The big panther knew the caribou. He knew that, with no reason other than their own caprice, the restless gray herds would drift away, forsaking the most congenial pastures, journey swiftly and eagerly league upon inconsequent league, and at last rest seemingly content with more perilous ranges and scanter forage, in a region remote and new.

He was an old beast, ripe in the craft of the hunt; and the caribou had done just what he knew in his heart they were likely to do. Nevertheless, because the head waters of the Upsalquitch were much to his liking, — the best hunting-ground, indeed, that he had ever found, — he had hoped for a miracle; he had grown to expect that these caribou would stay where they were well off. Their herds had thriven and increased during the five years of his guardianship. He had killed only for his needs, never for the lust of killing. He had kept all four-foot poachers far from his preserves; and no hunters cared to push their way to the inaccessible Upsalquitch while game was abundant on the Tobique and the Miramichi. He knew all these wilderness waters of northern New

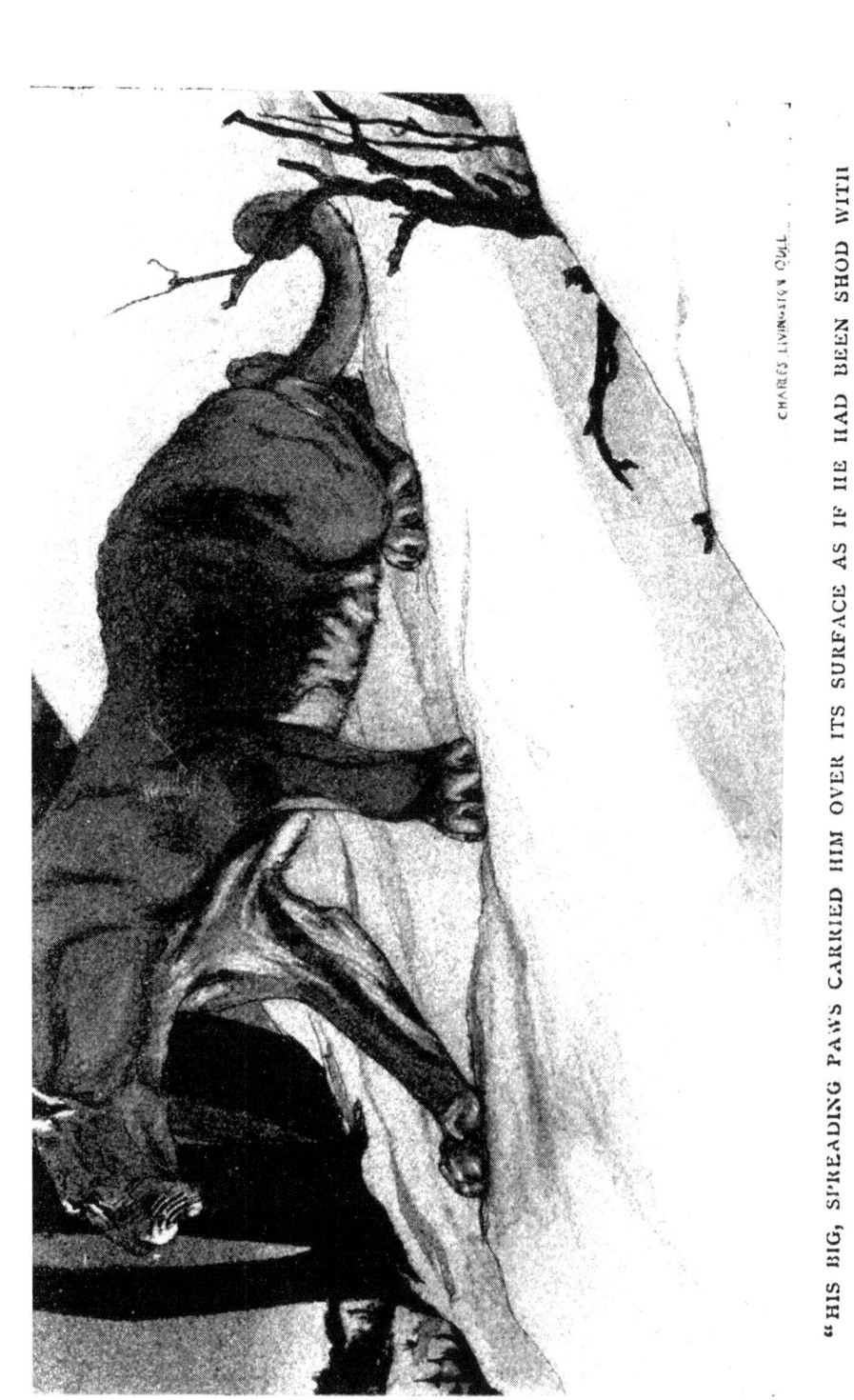

"HIS BIG, SPREADING PAWS CARRIED HIM OVER ITS SURFACE AS IF HE HAD BEEN SHOD WITH SNOW-SHOES."

Brunswick, having been born not far from the sources of the Nashwaak, and worked his way northward as soon as he was full-grown, to escape the hated neighbourhood of the settlements. He knew that his vanished caribou would find no other pastures so rich and safe as these which they had left. Nevertheless, they had left them. And now, after a month of rabbit meat, he would forsake them, too. He would move down westward, and either come upon the trail of his lost herds, or push over nearer to the St. John valley and find a country of deer.

The big panther was no lover of long journeyings, and he did not travel with the air of one bent on going far. He lingered much to hunt rabbits on the way; and wherever he found a lair to his liking he settled himself as if for a long sojourn. Nevertheless he had no idea of halting until he should reach a land of deer or caribou, and his steady drift to westward carried him far in the course of a week. The snow, though deep, was well packed by a succession of driving winds, and his big, spreading paws carried him over its surface as if he had been shod with snow-shoes.

By the end of a week, however, the continuous travelling on the unsubstantial diet of rabbit meat had begun to tell upon him. He was hungry and unsatisfied all the time, and his temper became abominable. Now and then in the night he was fortunate enough to surprise a red squirrel asleep in its nest, or a grouse rooting in its thicket; but these were mere atoms to his craving, and moreover their flesh belonged to the same pale order as that of his despised rabbits. When he came to a beaver village, the rounded domes of the houses dotting the snowy level of their pond, a faint steam of warmth and moisture arising from their ventilating holes like smoke, he sometimes so far forgot himself as to waste a few minutes in futile clawing at the roofs, though he knew well enough that several feet of mud, frozen to the solidity of rock, protected the savoury flat-tails from his appetite.

Once, in a deep, sheltered river-valley, where a strong rapid and a narrow deep cascade kept open a black pool of water all through the winter frost, his luck and his wits working together gained him a luncheon of fat porcupine. Tempted from its den by the unwonted warmth of noonday, the porcupine had crawled out upon a limb to observe how the winter was passing, and to sniff for signs of spring in the air. At the sight of the panther, who had climbed the tree and cut off its retreat, it bristled its black and white quills, whirled about on its branch, and eyed its foe with more anger than terror, confident in its pointed spines.

The panther understood and respected that fine array of needle-points, and ordinarily would have gone his way hungry rather than risk the peril of getting his paws and nose stuck full of those barbed weapons. But just now his cunning was very keenly on edge. He crawled within striking distance of the porcupine, and reached out his great paw, gingerly enough, to clutch the latter's unprotected face. Instantly the porcupine rolled itself into a bristling ball of needle-points and dropped to the ground below.

The panther followed at a single bound; but there was no need whatever of hurry. The porcupine lay on the snow, safely coiled up within its citadel of quills; and the panther lay down beside it, waiting for it to unroll. But after half an hour of this vain waiting, patience gave out and he began experimenting. Extending his claws to the utmost, so that the quill-points should not come in contact with the fleshy pads of his foot, he softly turned the porcupine over. Now it chanced that the hard, glassy snow whereon it lay sloped toward the open pool, and the bristling ball moved several feet down the slope. The panther's pale eyes gleamed with a sudden thought. He pushed the ball again, very, very delicately. Again, and yet again; till, suddenly, reaching a spot where the slope was steeper, it rolled of its own accord, and dropped with a splash into the icy current.

As it came to the surface the porcupine straightened itself out to swim for the opposite shore. But like a flash the panther's paw scooped under it, and the long keen claws caught it in the unshielded belly. Unavailing now were those myriad bristling spear-points; and when the panther continued his journey he left behind him but a skin of quills and some blood-stains on the snow, to tell the envious lucifees that one had passed that way who knew how to outwit the porcupine.

On the following day, about noon, he came across an astonishing and incomprehensible trail, at the first sight and scent of which the hair rose along his backbone.

The scent of the strange trail he knew, — and hated it, and feared it. It was the man-scent. But the shape and size of the tracks at first appalled him. He had seen men, and the footprints of men; but never men with feet so vast as these. The trail was perhaps an hour old. He sniffed at it and

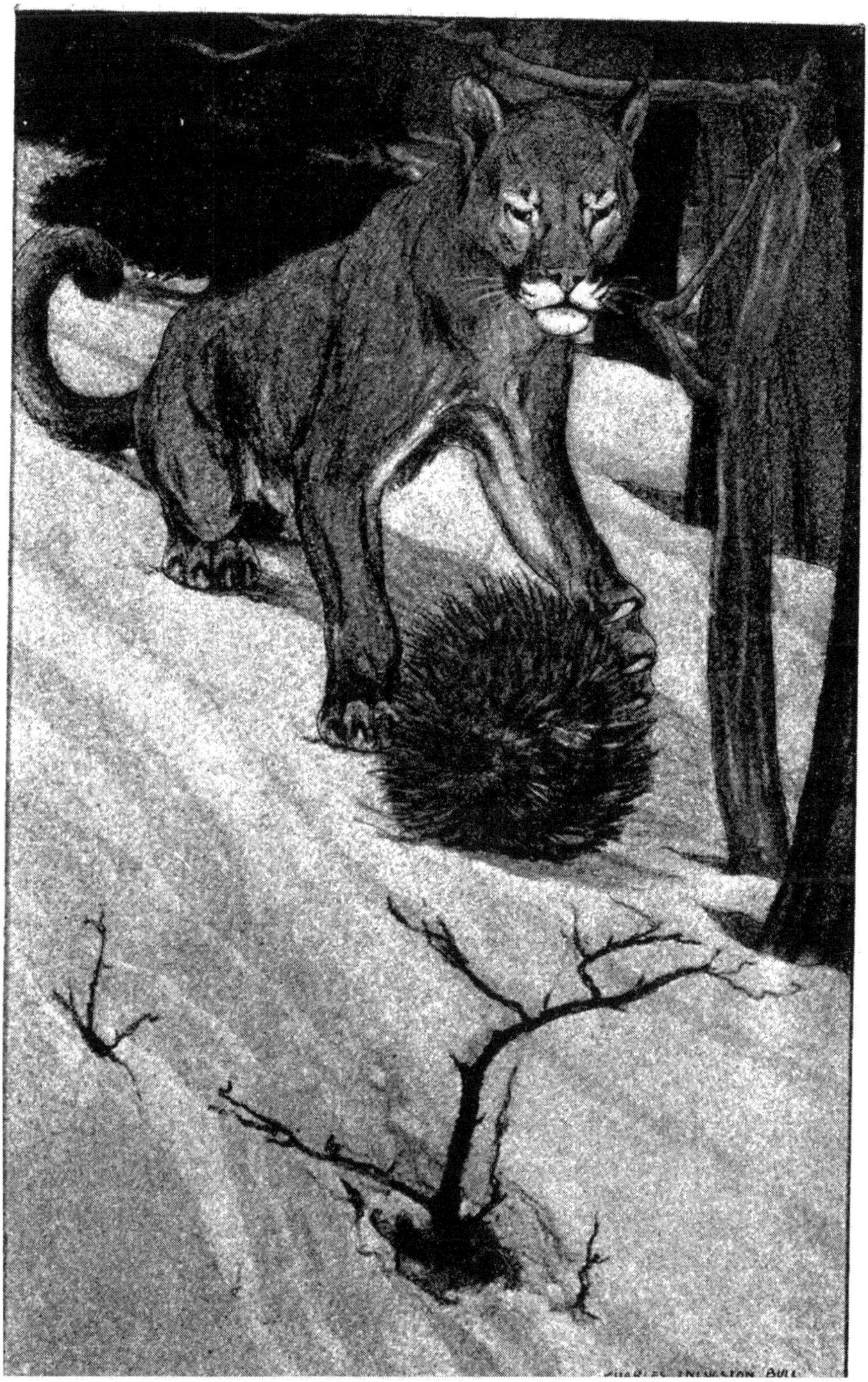

puzzled over it for a time; and then, perceiving that the man-scent clung only in a little depression about the centre of each track, concluded that the man who had made the track was no bigger than such men as he had seen. The rest of the trail was a puzzle, indeed, but it presently ceased to appal. Thereupon he changed his direction, and followed the man's trail at a rapid pace. His courage was not strung up to the pitch of resolving to attack this most dangerous and most dreaded of all creatures; but his hunger urged him insistently, and he hoped for some lucky chance of catching the man at a disadvantage. Moreover, it would soon be night, and he knew that with darkness his courage would increase, while that of the man — a creature who could not see well in the dark — should by all the laws of the wilderness diminish. He licked his lean chops at the thought of what would happen to the man unawares.

For some time he followed the trail at a shambling lope, every now and then dropping into an easy trot for the easement of the change. Occasionally he would stop and lie down for a few minutes at full length, to rest his overdriven lungs, being short-winded after the fashion of his kind. But when, toward sundown, when the shadows began to lengthen and turn blue upon the snow, and the western sky, through the spruce-tops, took upon a bitter wintry orange dye, he noticed that the trail was growing fresher. So strong did the man-scent become that he expected every moment to catch a glimpse of the man through the thicket. Thereupon he grew very cautious. No longer would he either lope or trot; but he crept forward, belly to the ground, setting down each paw with delicacy and precaution. He kept turning the yellow flame of his eyes from side to side continually, searching the undergrowth on every hand, and often looking back along his own track. He knew that men were sometimes inconceivably stupid, but at other times cunning beyond all the craft of the wood folk. He was not going to let himself become the hunted instead of the hunter, caught in the old device of the doubled trail.

At last, as twilight was gathering headway among the thickets, he was startled by a succession of sharp sounds just ahead of him. He stopped, and crouched motionless in his tracks. But presently he recognised and understood the sharp sounds, especially when they were followed by a crackling and snapping of dry branches. They were axe-strokes. He had heard them in the neighbourhood of the lumber camps, before his five years' retirement on the head waters of the Upsalquitch. With comprehension came new courage, — for the wild folk put human wisdom to shame in their judicious fear of what they do not understand. He crept a little nearer, and from safe hiding watched the man at his task of gathering dry firewood for the night. From time to time the man looked about him alertly, half suspiciously, as if he felt himself watched; but he could not discover the pale, cruel eyes that followed him unwinking from the depths of the hemlock thicket.

In a few minutes the panther was surprised to see the man take one of his heavy snow-shoes and begin digging vigorously at the snow. In a little while there was a circular hole dug so deep that when the man stood up in it little more than his head and shoulders appeared over the edge. Then he carried in a portion of the wood which he had cut, together with a big armful of spruce boughs; and he busied himself for awhile at the bottom of the hole, his head appearing now and then, but only for a moment. The panther was filled with curiosity, but restrained himself from drawing nearer to investigate. Then, when it had grown so dark that he was about to steal from his hiding and creep closer, suddenly there was a flash of light, and smoke and flame arose from the hole, throwing a red, revealing glare on every covert; and the panther, his lips twitching and his hair rising, shrank closer into his retreat.

The smoke, and the scent of the burning sticks, killed the scent of the man in the panther's nostrils. But presently there was a new scent, warm, rich, and appetising. The panther did not know it, but he liked it. It was the smell of frying bacon. Seeing that the man was much occupied over the fire, the hungry beast made a partial circuit of the camp-fire, and noiselessly climbed a tree whence he could look down into the mysterious hole.

From this post of vantage he watched the man make his meal, smoke his pipe, replenish the fire, and finally, rolling himself in his heavy blanket, compose himself to sleep. Then, little by little, the panther crept nearer. He feared the fire; but the fire soon began to die down, and he despised it as he saw it fading. He crept out upon a massive hemlock limb, almost overlooking the hole, but screened by a veil of fine green branches. From this post he could spring upon the sleeper at one bound, — as soon as he could make up his mind to the audacious enterprise. He feared the man, even asleep; in fact, he stood in strange awe of the helpless, slumbering form. But little by little he began to realise that he feared his own hunger more. Lower and lower sank the fainting fire; and he resolved that as soon as the sleeper should stir in his sleep, beginning to awake, he would spring. But the sleeper slept unstirring; and so the panther, equally unstirring, watched.

II.

A little beyond the camp-fire where the man lay sleeping under those sinister eyes, rose the slopes of a wooded ridge. The ridge was covered with a luxuriant second growth of birch, maple, Canada fir, moose-wood, and white spruce, the ancient forest having fallen years before under the axes of the lumbermen. Here on the ridge, where the food they loved was abundant, a buck, with his herd of does and fawns, had established his winter "yard." With their sharp, slim hoofs which cut deep into the snow, if the deer were compelled to seek their food at large they would find themselves at the mercy of every foe as soon as the snow lay deep enough to impede their running. It is their custom, therefore, at the beginning of winter, to select a locality where the food supply will not fail them, and intersect the surface of the snow in every direction with an inextricable labyrinth of paths. These paths are kept well trodden, whatever snow may fall. If straightened out they would reach for many a league. To unravel their intricacies is a task to which only the memories of their makers are equal, and along them the deer flee like wraiths at any alarm. If close pressed by an enemy they will leap, light as birds, from one deep path to another, leaving no mark on the intervening barrier of snow, and breaking the trail effectually. Thus when the snow lies deep, the yard becomes their spacious citadel, and the despair of pursuing lynx or panther. A herd of deer well yarded, under the leadership of an old and crafty buck, will come safe and sleek through the fiercest wilderness winter.

The little herd which occupied this particular yard chanced to be feeding, in the glimmer of the winter twilight, very near the foot of the ridge, when suddenly a faint red glow, stealing through the branches, caught the old buck's eye. There was a quick stamp of warning, and on the instant the herd turned to statues, their faces all one way, their sensitive ears, vibrating nostrils, and wide attentive eyes all striving to interpret the prodigy. They were a herd of the deep woods. Not one of them had ever been near the settlements. Not even the wise old leader had ever seen a fire. This light, when the sun had set and no moon held the sky, was inexplicable

But to the deer a mystery means something to be solved. He has the perilous gift of curiosity. After a few minutes of moveless watching, the whole herd, in single file, began noiselessly threading the lower windings of the maze, drawing nearer and nearer to the strange light. When the first smell of the burning came to their nostrils they stopped again, but not for long. That smell was just another mystery to be looked into. At the smell of the frying pork they stopped again, this time for a longer period and with symptoms of uneasiness. To their delicate nerves there was something of a menace in that forbidding odour. But even so, it was to be investigated; and very soon they resumed their wary advance.

A few moments more and they came to a spot where, peering through a cover of spruce boughs, their keen eyes could see the hole in the snow, the camp-fire, and the man seated beside it smoking his pipe. It was all very wonderful; but instinct told them it was perilous, and the old buck decided that the information they had acquired was sufficient for all practical purposes of a deer's daily life. He would go no nearer. The whole herd stood there for a long time, forgetting to eat, absorbed in the novelty and wonder of the scene.

The whole herd, did I say? There was one exception. To a certain young doe that fire was the most fascinating thing in life. It drew her. It hypnotised her. After a few minutes of stillness she could resist no longer. She pushed past the leader of the herd and stole noiselessly toward the shining lovely thing. The old buck signalled her back, — first gently, then angrily; but she had grown forgetful of the laws of the herd. She had but one thought, to get nearer to the camp-fire, and drench her vision in the entrancing glow.

Nevertheless, for all her infatuation, she forgot not her ancestral gift of prudence. She went noiselessly as a shadow, drifting, pausing, listening, sniffing the air, concealing herself behind every cover. The rest of the herd gazed after her with great eyes of resignation, then left her to her wayward will and resumed their watching of the camp-fire. When one member of a herd persists in disobeying orders, the rest endure with equanimity whatever fate may befall her.

Step by step, as if treading on egg-shells, the

"STOLE NOISELESSLY TOWARD THE SHINING LOVELY THING."

fascinated doe threaded the path till she came to the lowest limit of the yard. From that point the path swerved back up the ridge, forsaking the ruddy glow. The doe paused, hesitating. She was still too far from the object of her admiration and wonder; but she feared the deep snow. Her irresolution soon passed, however. Getting behind a thick hemlock, she cautiously raised herself over the barrier and made straight for the camp-fire.

Packed as the snow was, her light weight enabled her to traverse it without actually floundering. She sank deep at every step, but had perfect control of her motions, and made no more sound than if she had been a bunch of fur blown softly over the surface. Her absorption and curiosity, moreover, did not lead her to omit any proper precaution of woodcraft. As she approached the fire she kept always in the dense, confusing, shifting shadows which a camp-fire casts in the forest. These fitful shadows were a very effectual concealment.

At last she found herself so close to the fire that only a thicket of young spruce divided her from the edge of the hole.

Planting herself rigidly, her gray form an indeterminate shadow among the blotches and streaks of shadow, her wide mild eyes watched the man with intensest interest, as he knocked out his pipe, mended the fire, and rolled himself into his blanket on the spruce boughs. When she saw that he was asleep, she presently forgot about him. Her eyes returned to the fire and fixed themselves upon it. The veering, diminishing flames held her as by sorcery. All else was forgotten, — food, foes, and the herd alike, — as she stared with childlike eagerness at the bed of red coals. The pupils of her eyes kept alternately expanding and contracting, as the glow in the coals waxed and waned under the fluctuating breath of passing airs.

III.

Very early that same morning, a brown and grizzled chopper in Nicholson's camp, having obtained a brief leave of absence from the Boss, had started out on his snow-shoes for a two days' tramp to the settlements. He had been seized the night before with a sudden and irresistible homesickness. Shrewd, whimsical, humourous, kind, ever ready to stand by a comrade, fearless in all the daunting emergencies which so often confront the lumbermen in their strenuous calling, these sudden attacks of homesickness were his one and well-known failing in the eyes of his fellows. At least once in every winter he was sure to be so seized; and equally sure to be so favoured by the Boss. On account of his popularity in the camp, moreover, this favour excited no jealousy. It had come to be taken as a matter of course that Mac would go home for a few days if one of his "spells" came upon him. He was always "docked," to be sure, for the time of his absence, but as he never stayed away more than a week, his little holiday made no very serious breach in his roll when pay-day came.

Though not a hunter, the man was a thorough woodsman. He knew the woods, and the furtive inhabitants of them; and he loved to study their ways. Trails, in particular, were a passion with him, and he could read the varying purposes of the wild things by the changes in their footprints on the snow. He was learned, too, in the occult ways of the otter, whom few indeed are cunning enough to observe; and he had even a rudimentary knowledge of the complex vocabulary of the crow. He had no care to kill the wild things, great or small; yet he was a famous marksman, with his keen gray eye and steady hand. And he always carried a rifle on his long, solitary tramps.

He had two good reasons for carrying the rifle. The first of these was the fact that he had never seen a panther, and went always in the hope of meeting one. The stories which he had heard of them, current in all the lumber camps of northern New Brunswick, were so conflicting that he could not but feel uncertain as to the terms on which the encounter was likely to take place. The only point on which he felt assured was that he and the panther would some day meet, in spite of the fact that the great cat had grown so scarce in New Brunswick that some hunters declared it was extinct. The second reason was that he had a quarrel with all lucifees or lynxes, — "Injun devils," he called them. Once when he was a baby, just big enough to sit up when strapped into his chair, a lucifee had come and glared at him with fierce eyes through the doorway of his lonely backwoods cabin. His mother had come rushing from the cow-shed, just in time; and the lucifee, slinking off to the woods, had vented his disappointment in a series of soul-curdling screeches. The memory of this terror was a scar in his heart, which time failed to efface. He grew up to hate all lucifees; and from the day when he learned to handle a gun he was always ready to hunt them.

On this particular day of his life he had travelled all the morning without adventure, his face set eagerly toward the west. Along in the afternoon he was once or twice surprised by a creeping sensation along his backbone and in the roots of the hair on his neck. He stopped and peered about him searchingly, with a feeling that he was followed. But he had implicit faith in his eyesight; and when that revealed no menace he went onward reassured.

But when the diversion of gathering firewood and digging the hole that served him for a camp came to an end, and he stooped to build his camp-fire, that sensation of being watched came over him again. It was so strong that he straightened up sharply, and scrutinised every thicket within eyeshot. Thereafter, though he could see nothing to justify his curious uneasiness, the sensation kept recurring insistently all the time that he was occupied in cooking and eating his meal. When at last he was ready to turn in for his brief night's sleep, — he planned to be afoot again before dawn, — he heaped his frugal camp-fire a little higher than usual, and took the quite unwonted precaution of laying his rifle within instant grasp of his hand.

In spite of these vague warnings, wherein his instinct showed itself so much more sagacious than his reason, he fell asleep at once. His wholesome drowsiness, in that clear and vital air, was not to be denied. But once deep asleep, beyond the vacillation of ordered thought and the obstinacies of will, his sensitive intuitions reasserted themselves. They insisted sharply on his giving heed to their warnings; and all at once he found himself wide awake with not a vestige of sleep's heaviness left in his brain.

With his trained woodcraft, however, he knew that it was some peril that had thus awakened him, and he gave no sign of his waking. Without a movement, without a change in his slow, deep breathing, he half opened his eyes and scanned the surrounding trees through narrowed lids.

Presently he caught a glimmer of big, soft, round eyes gazing at him through a tangle of spruce boughs. *Were* they gazing at him? No, it was the fire that held their harmless attention. He guessed the owner of those soft eyes; and in a moment or two he was able to discern dimly the lines of the deer's head and neck.

His first impulse was to laugh impatiently at his own folly. Had he been enduring all these creepy apprehensions because an inquisitive doe had followed him? Had his nerves grown so sensitive that the staring of a chipmunk or a rabbit had power to break his sleep? But while these thoughts rushed through his brain his body lay still as before, obedient to the subtle dictates of his instinct. His long study of the wild things had taught him much of their special wisdom. He swept his glance around the dim-lit aisle as far as he could without perceptibly turning his head — and met the lambent blue-green gaze of the watching panther!

Through the thin veil of the hemlock twigs, he saw the body of the animal, gathered for the spring, and realised with a pang that the long expected had not arrived in just the form he would have chosen. He knew better than to reach for his rifle, — because he knew that the least movement of head or hand would be the signal for the launching of that fatal leap. There was nothing to do but wait, and keep motionless, and think.

The strain of that waiting was unspeakable, and under it the minutes seemed hours. But just as he was beginning to think he could stand it no longer, a brand in the fire burned through and broke smartly. Flames leapt up, with a shower of sparks, — and the panther, somewhat startled, drew back and shifted his gaze. It was but for an instant, but in that instant the man had laid hold of his rifle, drawn it to him, and got it into a position where one more swift movement would enable him to shoot.

But not the panther only had been startled by the breaking brand, the leaping flame. The young doe had leapt backward, so that a great birch trunk cut off her view of the fire. The first alarm gone by, she moved to recover her post of vantage. Very stealthily and silently she moved, — but the motion caught the panther's eye.

The man noted a change in the direction of the beast's gaze, a change in the light of his eyeballs. There was no more hate in them, no more doubt and dread; only hunger, and eager triumph. As softly as an owl's wings move through the coverts, the great beast drew back, and started to descend from the tree. He would go stalk deer, drink warm deer's blood, and leave the dangerous sleeper to his dreams.

But the man considered. Panthers were indeed very few in New Brunswick, and undeniably interesting. But he loved the deer; and to this particular doe he felt that he perhaps owed his life. The debt should be paid in full.

As the panther turned to slip down the trunk of the tree, the man sat up straight. He took careful but almost instantaneous aim, at a point just behind the beast's fore-shoulder. At the report the great body fell limp, a huddled heap of fur and long bared fangs. The man sprang to his feet and stirred the camp-fire to a blaze. And the doe, her heart pounding with panic, her curiosity all devoured in consuming terror, went crashing off through the bushes.

WHEN TWILIGHT FALLS ON THE STUMP LOTS

When Twilight Falls on the Stump Lots

THE wet, chill first of the spring, its blackness made tender by the lilac wash of the afterglow, lay upon the high, open stretches of the stump lots. The winter-whitened stumps, the sparse patches of juniper and bay just budding, the rough-mossed hillocks, the harsh boulders here and there up-thrusting from the soil, the swampy hollows wherein a coarse grass began to show green, all seemed anointed, as it were, to an ecstasy of peace by the chrism of that paradisal colour. Against the lucid immensity of the April sky the thin tops of five or six soaring ram-pikes aspired like violet flames. Along the skirts of the stump lots a fir wood reared a ragged-crested wall of black against the red amber of the horizon.

Late that afternoon, beside a juniper thicket not far from the centre of the stump lots, a young black and white cow had given birth to her first calf. The little animal had been licked assiduously by the mother's caressing tongue till its colour began to show of a rich dark red. Now it had struggled to its feet, and, with its disproportionately long, thick legs braced wide apart, was beginning to nurse. Its blunt wet muzzle and thick lips tugged eagerly, but somewhat blunderingly as yet, at the unaccustomed teats; and its tail lifted, twitching with delight, as the first warm streams of mother milk went down its throat. It was a pathetically awkward, unlovely little figure, not yet advanced to that youngling winsomeness which is the heritage, to some degree and at some period, of the infancy of all the kindreds that breathe upon the earth. But to the young mother's eyes it was the most beautiful of things. With her head twisted far around, she nosed and licked its heaving flanks as it nursed; and between deep, ecstatic breathings she uttered in her throat low murmurs, unspeakably tender, of encouragement and caress. The delicate but pervading flood of sunset colour had the effect of blending the ruddy-hued calf into the tones of the landscape; but the cow's insistent blotches of black and white stood out sharply, refusing to harmonise. The drench of violet light was of no avail to soften their staring contrasts. They made her vividly conspicuous across the whole breadth of the stump lots, to eyes that watched her from the forest coverts.

The eyes that watched her — long, fixedly, hungrily — were small and red. They belonged to a lank she-bear, whose gaunt flanks and rusty coat proclaimed a season of famine in the wilderness. She could not see the calf, which was hidden by a hillock and some juniper scrub; but its presence was very legibly conveyed to her by the mother's solicitous watchfulness. After a motionless scrutiny from behind the screen of fir branches, the lean bear stole noiselessly forth from the shadows into the great wash of violet light. Step by step, and very slowly, with the patience that endures because confident of its object, she crept toward that oasis of mothering joy in the vast emptiness of the stump lots. Now crouching, now crawling, turning to this side and to that, taking advantage of every hollow, every thicket, every hillock, every aggressive stump, her craft succeeded in eluding even the wild and menacing watchfulness of the young mother's eyes.

The spring had been a trying one for the lank she-bear. Her den, in a dry tract of hemlock wood some furlongs back from the stump lots, was a snug little cave under the uprooted base of a lone pine, which had somehow grown up among the alien hemlocks only to draw down upon itself at last, by its superior height, the fury of a passing hurricane. The winter had contributed but scanty snowfall to cover the bear in her sleep; and the March thaws, unseasonably early and ardent, had called her forth to activity weeks too soon. Then frosts had come with belated severity, sealing away the budding tubers, which are the bear's chief dependence for spring diet; and worst of all, a long stretch of intervale meadow by the neighbouring river, which had once been rich in ground-nuts, had been ploughed up the previous spring and subjected to the producing of oats and corn. When she was feeling the pinch of meagre rations, and when the fat which a liberal autumn of blueberries had laid up about her ribs was getting as shrunken as the last snow in the thickets, she gave birth to two hairless and hungry little cubs. They were very blind, and ridiculously small to be born of so big a mother; and having so much growth to make during the next few months, their appetites were immeasurable. They tumbled, and squealed, and tugged at their mother's teats, and grew astonishingly, and made huge haste to cover their bodies with fur of a soft and silken black; and all this vitality of theirs made a strenuous demand upon their mother's milk. There were no more bee-trees left in the neighbourhood. The long wanderings which she was forced to take in her search for roots and tubers were in themselves a drain upon her nursing powers. At last, reluctant though she was to attract the hostile notice of the settlement, she found herself forced to hunt on the borders of the sheep pastures. Before all else in life was it important to her that these two tumbling little ones in the den should not go hungry. Their eyes were open now — small and dark and whimsical, their ears quaintly large and inquiring for their roguish little faces. Had she not been driven by the unkind season to so much hunting and foraging, she would have passed near all her time rapturously in the den under the pine root, fondling those two soft miracles of her world.

With the killing of three lambs — at widely scattered points, so as to mislead retaliation — things grew a little easier for the harassed bear; and presently she grew bolder in tampering with the creatures under man's protection. With one swift, secret blow of her mighty paw she struck down a young ewe which had strayed within reach of her hiding-place. Dragging her prey deep into the woods, she fared well upon it for some days, and was happy with her growing cubs. It was just when she had begun to feel the fasting which came upon the exhaustion of this store that, in a hungry hour, she sighted the conspicuous markings of the black and white cow.

It is altogether unusual for the black bear of the eastern woods to attack any quarry so large as a cow, unless under the spur of fierce hunger or fierce rage. The she-bear was powerful beyond her fellows. She had the strongest possible incentive to bold hunting, and she had lately grown confident beyond her wont. Nevertheless, when she began her careful stalking of this big game which she coveted, she had no definite intention of forcing a battle with the cow. She had observed that cows, accustomed to the protection of man, would at times leave their calves asleep and stray off some distance in their pasturing. She had even seen calves left all by themselves in a field, from morning till night, and had wondered at such negligence in their mothers. Now she had a confident idea that sooner or later the calf would lie down to sleep, and the young mother roam a little wide in search of the scant young grass. Very softly, very self-effacingly, she crept nearer step by step, following up the wind, till at last, undiscovered, she was crouching behind a thick patch of juniper, on the slope of a little hollow not ten paces distant from the cow and the calf.

By this time the tender violet light was fading to a grayness over hillock and hollow; and with the deepening of the twilight the faint breeze, which had been breathing from the northward, shifted suddenly and came in slow, warm pulsations out of the south. At the same time the calf, having nursed sufficiently, and feeling his baby legs tired of the weight they had not yet learned to carry, laid himself down. On this the cow shifted her position. She turned half round, and lifted her head high. As she did so a scent of peril was borne in upon her fine nostrils. She recognised it instantly. With a snort of anger she sniffed again; then stamped a challenge with her fore hoofs, and levelled the lance-points of her horns toward the menace. The next moment her eyes, made keen by the fear of love, detected the black outline of the bear's head through the coarse screen of the juniper. Without a second's hesitation, she flung up her tail, gave a short bellow, and charged.

The moment she saw herself detected, the bear rose upon her hindquarters; nevertheless she was in a measure surprised by the sudden blind fury of the attack. Nimbly she swerved to avoid it, aiming at the same time a stroke with her mighty forearm, which, if it had found its mark, would have smashed her adversary's neck. But as she struck out, in the act of shifting her position, a depression of the ground threw her off her balance. The next instant one sharp horn caught her slantingly in the flank, ripping its way upward and inward, while the mad impact threw her upon her back.

Grappling, she had her assailant's head and shoulders in a trap, and her gigantic claws cut through the flesh and sinew like knives; but at the desperate disadvantage of her position she could inflict no disabling blow. The cow, on the other hand, though mutilated and streaming with blood, kept pounding with her whole massive weight, and with short tremendous shocks crushing the breath from her foe's ribs.

Presently, wrenching herself free, the cow drew off for another battering charge; and as she did so the bear hurled herself violently down the slope, and gained her feet behind a dense thicket of bay shrub. The cow, with one eye blinded and the other obscured by blood, glared around for her

"SHE STRUGGLED STRAIGHT TOWARD THE DEN THAT HELD HER YOUNG."

in vain, then, in a panic of mother terror, plunged back to her calf.

Snatching at the respite, the bear crouched down, craving that invisibility which is the most faithful shield of the furtive kindred. Painfully, and leaving a drenched red trail behind her, she crept off from the disastrous neighbourhood. Soon the deepening twilight sheltered her. But she could not make haste; and she knew that death was close upon her.

Once within the woods, she struggled straight toward the den that held her young. She hungered to die licking them. But destiny is as implacable as iron to the wilderness people, and even this was denied her. Just a half score of paces from the lair in the pine root, her hour descended upon her. There was a sudden redder and fuller gush upon the trail; the last light of longing faded out of her eyes; and she lay down upon her side.

The merry little cubs within the den were beginning to expect her, and getting restless. As the night wore on, and no mother came, they ceased to be merry. By morning they were shivering with hunger and desolate fear. But the doom of the ancient wood was less harsh than its wont, and spared them some days of starving anguish; for about noon a pair of foxes discovered the dead mother, astutely estimated the situation, and then, with the boldness of good appetite, made their way into the unguarded den.

As for the red calf, its fortune was ordinary. Its mother, for all her wounds, was able to nurse and cherish it through the night; and with morning came a searcher from the farm and took it, with the bleeding mother, safely back to the settlement. There it was tended and fattened, and within a few weeks found its way to the cool marble slabs of a city market.

THE KING OF THE MAMOZEKEL

The King of the Mamozekel

WHEN the king of the Mamozekel barrens was born, he was one of the most ungainly of all calves, — a moose-calf.

In the heart of a tamarack swamp, some leagues south from Nictau Mountain, was a dry little knoll of hardwood and pine undiscovered by the hunters, out of the track of the hunting beasts. Neither lynx, bear, nor panther had tradition of it. There was little succulent undergrowth to tempt the moose and the caribou. But there the wild plum each summer fruited abundantly, and there a sturdy brotherhood of beeches each autumn lavished their treasure of three-cornered nuts; and therefore the knoll was populous with squirrels and grouse. Nature, in one of those whims of hers by which she delights to confound the studious naturalist, had chosen to keep this spot exempt from the law of blood and fear which ruled the rest of her domains. To be sure, the squirrels would now and then play havoc with a nest of grouse eggs, or, in the absence of their chisel-beaked parents, do murder on a nest of young golden-wings; but, barring the outbreaks of these bright-eyed incorrigible marauders, — bad to their very toes, and attractive to their plumy tail-tips, — the knoll in the tamarack swamp was a haven of peace amid the fierce but furtive warfare of the wilderness.

On this knoll, when the arbutus breath of the northern spring was scenting the winds of all the Tobique country, the king was born, — a moose-calf more ungainly and of mightier girth and limb than any other moose-calf of the Mamozekel. Never had his mother seen such a one, — and she a mother of lordly bulls. He was uncouth, to be sure, in any eyes but those of his kind, — with his high humped fore-shoulders, his long, lugubrious, overhanging snout, his big ears set low on his big head, his little eyes crowded back toward his ears, his long, big-knuckled legs, and the spindling, lank diminutiveness of his hindquarters. A grotesque figure, indeed, and lacking altogether in that pathetic, infantile winsomeness which makes even little pigs attractive. But any one who knew about moose would have said, watching the huge baby struggle to his feet and stand with sturdy legs well braced, "There, if bears and bullets miss him till his antlers get full spread, is the king of the Mamozekel." Now, when his mother had licked him dry, his coat showed a dark, very sombre, cloudy, secretive brown, of a hue to be quite lost in the shadows of the fir and hemlock thickets, and to blend consummately with the colour of the tangled alder trunks along the clogged banks of the Mamozekel.

The young king's mother was perhaps the biggest and most morose cow on all the moose ranges of northern New Brunswick. She assuredly had no peer on the barrens of the upper Tobique country. She was also the craftiest. That was the reason why, though she was dimly known and had been blindly hunted all the way from Nictau Lake, over Mamozekel, and down to Blue Mountain on the main Tobique, she had never felt a bullet wound, and had come to be regarded by the backwoods hunters with something of a superstitious awe. It was of her craft, too, that she had found this knoll in the heart of the tamarack swamp, and had guarded the secret of it from the herds. Hither, at calving time, she would come by cunningly twisted trails. Here she would pass the perilous hours in safety, unharassed by the need of watching against her stealthy foes. And when once she had led her calf away from the retreat, she never returned to it, save alone, and in another year.

For three days the great cow stayed upon the knoll, feeding upon the overhanging branch tips of mountain-ash and poplar. This was good fodder, for buds and twigs were swollen with sap, and succulent. In those three days her sturdy young calf made such gains in strength and stature that he would have passed in the herd for a calf of two weeks' growth. In mid-afternoon of the third day she led the way down from the knoll and out across the quaking glooms of the tamarack swamp. And the squirrels in the budding branches chattered shrill derision about their going.

The way led through the deepest and most perilous part of the swamp; but the mother knew the safe trail in all its windings. She knew where the yielding surface of moss with black pools on either side was not afloat on fathomless ooze, but supported by solid earth or a framework of ancient tree roots. She shambled onward at a very rapid walk, which forced the gaunt calf at her heels to break now and then into the long-striding, tireless trot which is the heritage of his race.

For perhaps an hour they travelled. Then, in a little, partly open glade where the good sound earth rose up sweet from the morass, and the mountain-ash, the viburnum, and the moose-wood grew thinly, and the ground was starred with spring blooms, — painted trillium and wake-robin, claytonia and yellow dog-tooth and wind-flower, — they stopped. The calf, tired from his first journeying, nursed fiercely, twitching his absurd stub of a tail, butting at his mother's udder with such discomforting eagerness that she had to rebuke him by stepping aside and interrupting his meal. After several experiences of this kind he took the hint, and put curb upon his too robust impatience. The masterful spirit of a king is liable to inconvenience its owner if exercised prematurely.

By this time the pink light of sunset was beginning to stain the western curves of branch and stem and bud, changing the spring coolness of the place into a delicate riot of fairy colour and light, intervolving form. Some shadows deepened, while others disappeared. Certain leaves and blossoms and pale limbs stood out with a clearness almost startling, suddenly emphasised by the level rays, while others faded from view. Though there was no wind, the changed light gave an effect of noiseless movement in the glade. And in the midst of this gathering enchantment the mother moose set herself to forage for her own meal.

Selecting a slim young birch-tree, whose top was

thick with twigs and greening buds, she pushed against it with her massive chest till it bent nearly to the ground. Then straddling herself along it, she held it down securely between her legs, moved forward till the succulent top was within easy reach, and began to browse with leisurely jaws and selective reachings out of her long, discriminating upper lip. The calf stood close by, watching with interest, his legs sympathetically spread apart, his head swung low from his big shoulders, his great ears swaying slowly backward and forward, not together, but one at a time. When the mother had finished feeding, there were no buds, twigs or small branches left on the birch sapling; and the sunset colours had faded out of the glade. With dusk a chilly air breathed softly through the trees, and the mother led the way into a clump of thick balsam firs near the edge of the good ground. In the heart of the thicket she lay down for the night, facing away from the wind; and the calf, quick in perception as in growth, lay down close beside her in the same position. He did not know at the time the significance of the position, but he had a vague sense of its importance. He was afterward to learn that enemies were liable to approach his lair in the night, and that as long as he slept with his back to the

"THE CALF STOOD CLOSE BY, WATCHING WITH INTEREST."

wind, he could not be taken unawares. The wind might be trusted to bring to his marvellous nostrils timely notice of danger from the rear; while he could depend upon his eyes and his spacious, sensitive, unsleeping ears to warn him of anything ascending against the wind to attack him in front.

At the very first suggestion of morning the two light sleepers arose. In the dusk of the fir thicket the hungry calf made his meal. Then they came forth into the grayness of the spectral spring dawn, and the great cow proceeded as before to breast down a birch sapling for fodder. Before the sun was fairly up, they left the glade and resumed their journey across the swamp.

It was mid-morning of a sweet-aired, radiant day when they emerged from the swamp. Now, through a diversified country of thick forests and open levels, the mother moose swung forward on an undeviating trail, perceptible only to herself. Presently the land began to dip. Then a little river appeared, winding through innumerable alders, with here and there a pond-like expansion full of young lily-leaves; and the future king of the Mamozekel looked upon his kingdom. But he did not recognise it. He cared nothing for the little river of alders. He was tired, and very hungry, and the moment his mother halted he ran up and nursed vehemently.

II.

Delicately filming with the first green, and spicy-fragrant, were the young birch-trees on the slopes about the Mamozekel water. From tree-top to tree-top, across the open spaces, the rain-birds called to each other with long falls of melody and sweetly insistent iteration. In their intervals of stillness, which came from time to time as if by some secret and preconcerted signal, the hush was beaded, as it were, with the tender and leisurely staccatos of the chickadees. The wild kindreds of the Tobique country were all happily busy with affairs of spring.

While the great cow was pasturing on birch-twigs, the calf rested, with long legs tucked under him, on the dry, softly carpeted earth beneath the branches of a hemlock. At this pleasant pasturage the mother moose was presently joined by her calf of the previous season, a sturdy bull-yearling, which ran up to her with a pathetic little bleat of delight, as if he had been very desolate and bewildered during the days of her strange absence. The mother received him with good-natured indifference, and went on pulling birch-tips. Then the yearling came over and eyed with curiosity the resting calf, — the first moose-calf he had ever seen. The king, unperturbed and not troubling himself to rise, thrust forward his spacious ears, and reached out a long inquiring nose to investigate the newcomer. But the yearling was in doubt. He drew back, planted his fore hoofs firmly, and lowered and shook his head, challenging the stranger to a butting bout. The old moose, which had kept wary eye upon the meeting, now came up and stood over her young, touching him once or twice lightly with her upper lip. Then, swinging her great head to one side, she glanced at the yearling, and made a soft sound in her throat. Whether this were warning or mere pertinent information, the yearling understood that his smaller kinsman was to be let alone, and not troubled with challenges. With easy philosophy, he accepted the situation, doubtless not concerned to understand it, and turned his thoughts to the ever fresh theme of forage.

Through the spring and summer the little family of three fed never far from the Mamozekel stream; and the king grew with astonishing speed. Of other moose families they saw little, for the mother, jealous and overbearing in her strength, would tolerate no other cows on her favourite range. Sometimes they saw a tall bull, with naked forehead, come down to drink or to pull lily-stems in the still pools at sunset. But the bull, feeling himself discrowned and unlordly in the absence of his antlers, paid no attention to either cows or calves. While waiting for autumn to restore to his forehead its superb palmated adornments, he was haughty and seclusive.

By the time summer was well established in the land, the moose-calf had begun to occupy himself diligently with the primer-lessons of life. Keeping much at his mother's head, he soon learned to pluck the tops of tall seeding grasses; though such low-growing tender herbage as cattle and horses love, he never learned to crop. His mother, like all his tribe, was too long in the legs and short in the neck to pasture close to the ground. He was early taught, however, what succulent pasturage of root and stem and leaf the pools of Mamozekel could supply; and early his sensitive upper lip acquired the wisdom to discriminate between the wholesome water-plants and such acrid, unfriendly growths as the water-parsnip and the spotted cowbane. Most pleasant the little family found it, in the hot, drowsy afternoons, to wade out into the leafy shallows and feed at leisure belly-deep in the cool, with no sound save their own comfortable splashings, or the shrill clatter of a kingfisher winging past up-stream.

Their usual feeding hours were just before sunrise, a little before noon, and again in the late afternoon, till dark. The rest of the time they would lie hidden in the deepest thickets, safe, but ever watchful, their great ears taking in and interpreting all the myriad fluctuating noises of the wilderness.

The hours of foraging were also — for the young king, in particular, whose food was mostly provided by his mother — the hours of lesson and the hours of play. In the pride of his growing strength he quickly developed a tendency to butt at everything and test his prowess. His yearling brother was always ready to meet his desires in this fashion, and the two would push against each other with much grunting, till at last the elder, growing impatient, would thrust the king hard back upon his haunches, and turn aside indifferently to his browsing. Little by little it became more difficult for the yearling to close the bout in this easy way; but he never guessed that in no distant day the contests would end in a very different manner. He did not know that, for a calf of that same spring, his lightly tolerated playfellow was big and strong and audacious beyond all wont of the wide-antlered kindred.

The young king was always athrill with curiosity.

full of interest in all the wilderness folk that chanced to come in his view. The shyest of the furtive creatures were careless about letting him see them, both his childishness and his race being guarantee of good will. Very soon, therefore, he became acquainted, in a distant, uncomprehending fashion, with the hare and the mink, the woodmouse and the muskrat; while the mother mallard would float amid her brood within a yard or two of the spot where he was pulling at the water-lilies.

One day, however, he came suddenly upon a porcupine which was crossing a bit of open ground, — came upon it so suddenly that the surly little beast was startled and rolled himself up into a round, bristling ball. This was a strange phenomenon indeed! He blew upon the ball, two or three hard noisy breaths from wide nostrils. Then he was so rash as to thrust at it, tentatively rather than roughly, with his inquisitive nose, — for he was most anxious to know what it meant. There was a quiver in the ball; and he jumped back, shaking his head, with two of the sharp spines sticking in his sensitive upper lip.

In pain and fright, yet with growing anger, he ran to his mother where she was placidly cropping a willow-top. But she was not helpful. She knew

"THE MOTHER MALLARD WOULD FLOAT AMID HER BROOD."

nothing of the properties of porcupine quills. Seeing what was the matter, she set the example of rubbing her nose smartly against a stump. The king did likewise. Now, for burrs, this would have been all very well; but porcupine quills — the malignant little intruders throve under such treatment, and worked their way more deeply into the tender tissues. Smarting and furious, the young monarch rushed back with the purpose of stamping that treacherous ball of spines to fragments under his sharp hoofs. But the porcupine, meanwhile, had discreetly climbed a tree, whence it looked down with scornful red eyes, bristling its barbed armory, and daring the angry calf to come up and fight. For days thereafter the young king suffered from a nose so hot and swollen that it was hard for him to browse, and almost impossible for him to nurse. Then came relief, as the quills worked their way through, one dropping out, and the other getting chewed up with a lily-root. But the young moose never forgot his grudge against the porcupine family; and catching one, years after, in a poplar sapling, he bore the sapling down and trod his enemy to bits. In his wrath, however, he did not forget the powers and properties of the quills. He took good care that none should pierce the tender places of his feet.

Some weeks after his meeting with the porcupine, when his nose and his spirits together had quite recovered, he made a new acquaintance. The moose family had by this time worked much farther up the Mamozekel, into a region of broken ground, and steep up-thrusts of rock. One day, while investigating the world at a little distance from his mother and brother, he saw a large, curious-looking animal at the top of a rocky slope. It was a light brown-gray in colour, with a big, round face, high-tufted ears, round, light, cold eyes, long whiskers brushed back from under its chin, very long, sharp teeth displayed in its snarlingly open jaws, and big round pads of feet. The lynx glared at the young king, scornfully unacquainted with his kingship. And the young king stared at the lynx with lively, unhostile interest. Then the lynx cast a wary glance all about, saw no sign of the mother moose (who was feeding on the other side of the rock), concluded that this was such an opportunity as he had long been looking for, and began creeping swiftly, stealthily, noiselessly, down the slope of rocks.

Any other moose-calf, though of thrice the young king's months, would have run away. But not so he. The stranger seemed unfriendly. He would try a bout of butting with him. He stamped his feet, shook his lowered head, snorted, and advanced a stride or two. At the same time, he uttered a harsh, very abrupt, bleating cry of defiance, the infantile precursor of what his mighty, forest-daunting bellow was to be in later years. The lynx, though he well knew that this ungainly youngster could not withstand his onslaught for a moment, was nevertheless astonished by such a display of spirit; and he paused for a moment to consider it. Was it possible that unguessed resources lay behind this daring? He would see.

It was a critical moment. A very few words more would have sufficed for the conclusion of this chronicle, but for the fact that the young king's bleat of challenge had reached other ears than those of the great lynx. The old moose, at her pasturing behind the rock, heard it too. Startled and anxious, she came with a rush to find out what it meant; and the yearling, full of curiosity, came at her heels. When she saw the lynx, the long hair on her neck stood up with fury, and with a roar she launched her huge, dark bulk against him. But for such an encounter the big cat had no stomach. He knew that he would be pounded into paste in half a minute. With a snarl, he sprang backward, as if his muscles had been steel springs suddenly loosed; and before his assailant was half-way up the slope, he was glaring down upon her from the safe height of a hemlock limb.

This, to the young king, seemed a personal victory. The mother's efforts to make him understand that lynxes were dangerous had small effect upon him; and the experience advanced him not at all in his hitherto unlearned lesson of fear.

Even he, however, for all his kingly heart, was destined to learn that lesson, — was destined to have it so seared into his spirit that the remembrance should, from time to time, unnerve, humiliate, defeat him, through half the years of his sovereignty.

It came about in this way, one blazing August afternoon.

The old moose and the yearling were at rest, comfortably chewing the cud in a spruce covert close to the water. But the king was in one of those restless fits which, all through his calfhood, kept driving him forward in quest of experience. The wind was almost still; but such as there was blew up stream. Up against it he wandered for a little way, and saw nothing but a woodchuck, which was a familiar sight to him. Then he turned and drifted carelessly down the wind. Having

The King of the Mamozekel 307

passed the spruce thicket, his nostrils received messages from his mother and brother in their quiet concealment. The scent was companion to him, and he wandered on. Presently it faded away from the faintly pulsing air. Still he went on.

Presently he passed a huge, half-decayed windfall, thickly draped in shrubbery and vines. No sooner had he passed than the wind brought him from this dense hiding-place a pungent, unfamiliar scent. There was something ominous in the smell, something at which his heart beat faster; but he was not afraid. He stopped at once, and moved back slowly toward the windfall, sniffing with curiosity, his ears alert, his eyes striving to pierce the mysteries of the thicket.

He moved close by the decaying trunk without solving the enigma. Then, as the wind puffed a thought more strongly, he passed by and lost the scent. At once he swung about to pursue the investigation; and at the same instant an intuitive apprehension of peril made him shudder, and shrink away from the windfall.

He turned not an instant too soon. What he saw was a huge, black, furry head and shoulders leaning over the windfall, a huge black paw, with knife-like claws, lifting for a blow that would break his back like a bulrush. He was already moving, already turning, and with his muscles gathered. That saved him. Quick as a flash of light he sprang, wildly. Just as quickly, indeed, came down the stroke of those terrific claws. But they fell short of their intended mark. As the young moose sprang into the air, the claws caught him slantingly on the haunch. They went deep, ripping hide and flesh almost to the bone, — a long, hideous wound. Before the blow could be repeated, the calf was far out of reach, bleating with pain and terror. The bear, much disappointed, peered after him with little red, malicious eyes, and greedily licked the sweet blood from his claws.

The next instant the mother moose burst from her thicket, the long hair of her neck and shoulders stiffly erect with rage. She had understood well enough that agonised cry of the young king. She paused but a second, to give him a hasty lick of reassurance, then charged down upon the covert around the windfall. She knew that only a bear could have done that injury; and she knew, without any help from ears, eyes, or nose, that the windfall was just the place for a bear's lying-in-wait. With an intrepidity beyond the boldest dreams of any other moose-cow on the Mamozekel, she launched herself crashing into the covert.

"BUT THEY FELL SHORT OF THEIR INTENDED MARK."

But her avenging fury found no bear to meet it. The bear knew well this mighty moose-cow, having watched her from many a hiding-place, and shrewdly estimated her prowess. He had effaced himself, melting away through the underwood as noiselessly and swiftly as a weasel. Plenty of the strong bear scent the old moose found in the covert, and it stung her to frenzy. She stamped and tore down the vines, and sent the rotten wood of the windfall flying in fragments. Then she emerged, powdered with débris, and roared and glared about for the enemy. But the wily bear was already far away, well burdened with discretion.

III.

In a few weeks the king's healthy flesh, assiduously licked by his mother, healed perfectly, leaving long, hairless scars upon his hide, which turned, in course of time, from livid to a leaden whitish hue. But while his flesh healed perfectly, his spirit was in a different case. Thenceforward, one great fear lurked in his heart, ready to leap forth at any instant — the fear of the bear. It was the only fear he knew, but it was a terrible one; and when, two months later, he again caught that pungent scent in passing a thicket, he ran madly for an hour before he recovered his wits and stole back, humiliated and exhausted, to his mother's pasture-grounds.

In the main, however, he was soon his old, bold, investigating self, his bulk and his sagacity growing vastly together. Ere the first frosts had crimsoned the maples and touched the birches to a shimmer of pale gold, he could almost hold his own by sheer strength against his yearling brother's weight, and sometimes, for a minute or two, worst him by feint and strategy. When he came, by chance, in the crisp, free-roving weather of the fall, upon other moose-calves of that year's birth, they seemed pygmies beside him, and gave way to him respectfully as to a yearling.

About this time he experienced certain qualms of loneliness, which bewildered him and took much of the interest out of life. His mother began to betray an unexpected indifference, and his childish heart missed her caresses. He was not driven away, but he was left to himself; while she would stride up and down the open, gravelly meadows by the water, sniffing the air, and at times uttering a short, harsh roar which made him eye her uneasily. One crisp night, when the round October moon wrought magic in the wilderness, he heard his mother's call answered by a terrific, roaring bellow,

The King of the Mamozekel 313

which made his heart leap. Then there was a crashing through the underbrush; and a tall bull strode forth into the light, his antlers spreading like oak branches from either side of his forehead. Prudence, or deference, or a mixture of the two, led the young king to lay aside his wonted inquisitiveness and withdraw into the thickets without attracting the notice of this splendid and formidable visitor. During the next few days he saw the big bull very frequently, and found himself calmly ignored. Prudence and deference continued their good offices, however, and he was careful not to trespass on the big stranger's tolerance during those wild, mad, magical autumn days.

One night, about the middle of October, the king saw from his thicket a scene which filled him with excitement and awe, swelled his veins almost to bursting, and made his brows ache, as if the antlers were already pushing to birth beneath the skin. It all came about in this fashion. His mother, standing out in the moonlight by the water, had twice with outstretched muzzle uttered her call, when it was answered not only by her mate, the tall bull, approaching along the shore, but by another great voice from up the hillside. Instantly the tall bull was in a rage. He rushed up to the cow, touched her with his nose, and then, after a succession of roars which were answered promptly from the hillside, he moved over to the edge of the open and began thrashing the bushes with his antlers. A great crashing of underbrush arose some distance away, and drew near swiftly; and in a few minutes another bull burst forth violently into the open. He was young and impetuous, or he would have halted a moment before leaving cover, and stealthily surveyed the situation. But not yet had years and overthrows taught him the ripe moose wisdom; and with a reckless heart he committed himself to the combat.

The newcomer had barely the chance to see where he was, before the tall bull was upon him. He wheeled in time, however, and got his guard down; but was borne back upon his haunches by the terrific shock of the charge. In a moment or two he recovered the lost ground, for youth had given him strength, if not wisdom; and the tall bull, his eyes flame-red with wrath, found himself fairly matched by this shorter, stockier antagonist.

The night forthwith became tempestuous with gruntings, bellowings, the hard clashing of antlers, the stamping of swift and heavy feet. The thin turf was torn up. The earthy gravel was sent flying from the furious hoofs. From his covert the young king strained eager eyes upon the fight, his sympathies all with the tall bull whom he had regarded reverently from the first moment he saw him. But as for the cow, she moved up from the waterside and looked on with a fine impartiality. What concerned her was chiefly that none but the bravest and strongest should be her mate,—a question which only fighting could determine. Her favour would go with victory.

As it appeared, the rivals were fairly matched in vigour and valour. But among moose, as among men, brains count in the end. When the tall bull saw that, in a matter of sheer brawn, the sturdy stranger might hold him, he grew disgusted at the idea of settling such a vital question by mere butting and shoving. The red rage faded in his eyes, and a colder light took its place. On a sudden, when his foe had given a mighty thrust, he yielded, slipped his horns from the lock, and jumped nimbly aside. The stranger lunged forward, almost stumbling to his knees.

This was the tall bull's opportunity. In a whirlwind of fury he thrust upon the enemy's flank, goring him, and bearing him down. The latter, being short and quick-moving, recovered his feet in a second, and wheeled to present his guard. But the tall bull was quick to maintain the advantage. He, too, had shifted ground; and now he caught his antagonist in the rear. There was no resisting such an attack. With hind legs weakly doubling under him, with the weight of doom descending upon his defenceless rump, the rash stranger was thrust forward, bellowing madly, and striving in vain to brace himself. His humiliation was complete. With staring eyes and distended nostrils he was hustled across the meadow and over the edge of the bank. With a huge splash, and carrying with him a shower of turf and gravel, he fell into the stream. Once in the water, and his courage well cooled, he did not wait for a glance at his snorting and stamping conqueror on the bank above, but waded desperately across, dripping, bleeding, crushed in spirit, — and vanished into the woods. In the thicket, the king's heart swelled as if the victory had been his own.

By and by, when the last of the leaves had fluttered down with crisp whisperings from the birch and ash, maple and poplar, and the first enduring snows were beginning to change the face of the world, the tall bull seemed to lay aside his haughtiness. He grew carelessly good-natured toward the young king and the yearling, and frankly took command of the little herd. As the snow deepened, he led the way northward toward the Nictau Lake and chose winter quarters on the wooded southward slopes of Bald Mountain, where there were hemlock groves for shelter and an abundance of young hardwood growth for browsing.

This leisurely migration was in the main uneventful, and left but one sharp impression on the young king's memory. On a wintry morning, when the sunrise was reaching long pink-saffron fingers across the thin snow, a puff of wind brought with it from a tangle of stumps and rocks a breath of that pungent scent so hateful to a moose's nostrils. The whole herd stopped; and the young king, his knees quaking under him and his eyes staring with panic, crowded close against his mother's flank. The tall bull stamped and bellowed his defiance to the enemy, — but the enemy, being discreet, made no reply whatever. It is probable, indeed, that he was preparing his winter quarters, and getting too drowsy to hear or heed the angry challenge; but if he did hear it no doubt he noiselessly withdrew himself till the dangerous travellers had gone by. In a few minutes the herd resumed its march, — the king keeping close to his mother's side, instead of in his proper place in the line.

The big-antlered bull now chose his site for the "yard," with "verge and room enough" for all contingencies. The "yard" was an ample acreage of innumerable winding paths, trodden ever deeper as the snows accumulated. These paths led to every spot of browse, every nook of shelter, at the same time twisting and crossing in a maze of intricacies. Thick piled the snows about the little herd, and the northern gales roared over the hemlocks, and the frost sealed the white world down into silence. But it was such a winter as the moose kin loved. No wolves or hunters came to trouble them, and the months passed pleasantly. When the days were lengthening and the hearts of all the wild folk beginning to dream of the yet unsignalled spring, the young king was astonished to see the great antlers of his leader fall off. Seeing that their owner left them lying unregarded on the snow, he went up and sniffed at them wonderingly, and pondered the incident long and vainly in his heart.

When the snows shrank away, departing with a sound of many waters, and spring returned to the Tobique country, the herd broke up. First the dis-antlered bull drifted off on his own affairs. Then the two-year-old went, with no word of reason or excuse. Though a well-grown young bull, he

"THICK PILED THE SNOWS ABOUT THE LITTLE HERD."

was now little larger or heavier than the king; and the king was now a yearling, with the stature and presence of a two-year-old. In a playful butting contest, excited by the joy of life which April put into their veins, he worsted his elder brother; and this, perhaps, though taken in good part, hastened the latter's going.

A few days later the old cow grew restless. She and the king turned their steps backward toward the Mamozekel, feeding as they went. Soon they found themselves in their old haunts, which the king remembered very well. Then one day, while the king slept without suspicion of evil, the old cow slipped away stealthily, and sought her secret refuge in the heart of the cedar swamp. When the king awoke, he found himself alone in the thicket.

All that day he was most unhappy. For some hours he could not eat, but strayed hither and thither, questing and wondering. Then, when hunger drove him to browse on the tender birch-twigs, he would stop every minute or two to call in his big, gruff, pathetic bleat, and look around eagerly for an answer. No answer came from the deserting mother, by this time far away in the swamp.

But there were ears in the wilderness that heard and heeded the call of the desolate yearling. A pair of hunting lynxes paused at the sound, licked their chops, and crept forward with a green light in their wide, round eyes.

Their approach was noiseless as thought,—but the king, on a sudden, felt a monition of their coming. Whirling sharply about, he saw them lurking in the underbrush. He recognised the breed. This was the same kind of creature which he had been ready to challenge in his first calfhood. No doubt, it would have been more prudent for him to withdraw; but he was in no mood for concession. His sore heart made him ill-tempered. His lonely bleat became a bellow of wrath. He stamped the earth, shook his head as if thrashing the underbrush with imaginary antlers, and then charged madly upon the astonished cats. This was no ordinary moose-calf, they promptly decided; and in a second they were speeding away with great bounds, gray shadows down the gray vistas of the wood. The king glared after them for a moment, and then went back to his feeding, greatly comforted.

It was four days before his mother came back, bringing a lank calf at her heels. He was glad to see her, and contentedly renewed the companionship; but in those four days he had learned full self-reliance, and his attitude was no longer that of the yearling calf. It had become that of the equal. As for the lank little newcomer, he viewed it with careless complaisance, and no more dreamed of playing with it than if it had been a frog or a chipmunk.

The summer passed with little more event for the king than his swift increase in stature. One lesson then learned, however, though but vaguely comprehended at the time, was to prove of incalculable value in after years. He learned to shun man, — not with fear, indeed, for he never learned to fear anything except bears, — but with aversion, and a certain half-disdainful prudence. It was as if he came to recognise in man the presence of powers which he was not anxious to put to trial, lest he should be forced to doubt his own supremacy.

It was but a slight incident that gave him the beginning of this valuable wisdom. As he lay ruminating one day beside his mother and the gaunt calf, in a spruce covert near the water, a strange scent was wafted in to his nostrils. It carried with it a subtle warning. His mother touched him with her nose, conveying a silent yet eloquent monition, and got upon her feet with no more sound than if she had been compact of thistle-down. From their thicket shelter the three stared forth, moveless and unwinking, ears forward, nostrils wide. Then a canoe with two men came into view, paddling lazily, and turning to land. To the king, they looked not dangerous; but every detail of them — their shape, motion, colour, and, above all, their ominous scent — stamped itself in his memory. Then, to his great surprise, his mother silently signalled the gravest and most instant menace, and forthwith faded back through the thicket with inconceivably stealthy motion. The king and the calf followed with like care, — the king, though perplexed, having faith in his mother's wise woodcraft. Not until they had put good miles between themselves and strange-smelling newcomers did the old moose call a halt; and from all this precaution the king realised that the mysterious strangers were something to be avoided by moose.

That summer the king saw nothing more of the man-creatures, — and he crossed the scent of no more bears. His great heart, therefore, found no check to its growing arrogance and courage. When the month of the falling leaves and the whirring partridge-coveys again came round, he felt a new pugnacity swelling in his veins, and found himself uttering challenges, he knew not why, with his yet half infantile bellow. When, at length, his mother began to pace the open meadow by the Mamozekel, and startle the moonlit silences with her mating call, he was filled with strange anger. But this was nothing to his rage when the calls were answered by a wide-antlered bull. This time the king refused to slink obsequiously to cover. He waited in the open; and he eyed the new wooer in a fashion so truculent that at length he attracted notice.

For his dignity, if not for his experience, this was most unfortunate. The antlered stranger noted his size, his attitude of insolence, and promptly charged upon him. He met the charge, in his insane audacity, but was instantly borne down. As he staggered to his feet he realised his folly, and turned to withdraw,—not in terror, but in acknowledgment of superior strength. Such a dignified retreat, however, was not to be allowed him. The big bull fell upon him again, prodding him cruelly. He was hustled ignominiously across the meadow, and into the bushes. Thence he fled, bleating with impotent wrath and shame.

In his humiliation he fled far down along the river,

through alder swamps which he had never traversed, by pools in which he had never pulled the lilies. Onward he pressed, intent on placing irrevocably behind him the scene of his chagrin.

At length he came out upon the fair river basin where the Mamozekel, the Serpentine, and the Nictau, tameless streams, unite to form the main Tobique. Here he heard the call of a young cow, — a voice thinner and higher than his mother's deep-chested notes. With an impulse which he did not understand, he pushed forward to answer the summons, no longer furtive, but noisily trampling the brush. Just then, however, a pungent smell stung his nostrils. There, not ten paces distant, was a massive black shape standing out in the moonlight. Panic laid grip upon his heart, chilling every vein. He wheeled, splashed across the shallow waters of the Nictau, and fled away northward on tireless feet.

That winter the king yarded alone, like a morose old bull, far from his domain of the Mamozekel. In the spring he came back, but restricted his range to the neighbourhood of the Forks. And he saw his mother no more.

That summer he grew his first antlers. As antlers, indeed, they were no great thing; but they started out bravely, a massive cylindrical bar

The King of the Mamozekel

thrusting forth laterally, unlike the pointing horns of deer and caribou, from either side of his forehead. For all this sturdy start, their spiking and palmation did not amount to much; but he was inordinately proud of them, rubbing off the velvet with care when it began to itch, and polishing assiduously at the hardened horn. By the time the October moon had come round again to the Tobique country, he counted these first antlers a weapon for any encounter; and, indeed, with his bulk and craft behind them, they were formidable.

It was not long before they were put to the test. One night, as he stood roaring and thrashing the bushes on the bluff overlooking the Forks, he heard the call of a young cow a little way down the shore. Gladly he answered. Gladly he sped to the tryst. Strange ecstasies, the madness of the night spell, and the white light's sorcery made his heart beat and his veins run sweet fire. But suddenly all this changed; for another roar, a taunting challenge, answered him; and another bull broke from covert on the other side of the sandy level where stood the young cow coquettishly eyeing both wooers.

The new arrival was much older than the king, and nobly antlered; but in matter of inches the young king was already his peer. In craft, arrogance, and self-confident courage the king had an advantage that outweighed the deficiency in antlers. The fury of his charge spelled victory from the first; and though the battle was prolonged, the issue was decided at the outset, as the interested young cow soon perceived. In about a half-hour it was all over. The wise white moon of the wilderness looked down understandingly upon the furrowed sandspit, the pleased young cow, and the king making diffident progress with his first wooing. Some distance down the river-bank, she caught glimpses of the other bull, whose antlers had not saved him, fleeing in shame, with bleeding flanks and neck, through the light-patched shadows of the forest.

IV.

During the next four years the king learned to grow such antlers as had never before been seen in all the Tobique country. So tall, impetuous, and masterful he grew, that the boldest bulls, recognising the vast reverberations of his challenge, would smother their wrath and slip noiselessly away from his neighbourhood. Rumours of his size and his great antlers in some way got abroad among the settlements; but so crafty was he in shunning men, — whom he did not really fear, and whom he was wont to study intently from safe coverts, — that there was never a hunter who could boast of having got a shot at him.

Once, and once only, did he come into actual, face to face conflict with the strange man-creature. It was one autumn evening, at the first of the season. By the edge of a little lake, he heard the call of a cow. Having already found a mate, he was somewhat inattentive, and did not answer; but something strange in the call made him suspicious, and he stole forward, under cover, to make an observation. The call was repeated, seeming to come from a little, rushy island, a stone's throw from shore. This time there came an answer, — not from the king, but from an eager bull rushing up from the outlet of the lake. The king listened, with some lazy interest, to the crashing and slashing of the impetuous approach, thinking that if the visitor were big enough to be worth while he would presently go out and thrash him. When the visitor did appear, however, bursting from the underbrush and striding boldly down to the water's edge, a strange thing happened. From the rushy island came a spurt of flame, a sharp detonating report. The bull jumped and wheeled in his tracks. Another report, and he dropped without a kick. As he lay in the pale light, close to the water, a canoe shot out from the rushy island and landed some distance from the body. Two men sprang out. They pulled up the canoe, leaving their rifles in it, and ran up to skin the prize.

The king in his hiding-place understood. This was what men could do, — make a strange, menacing sound, and kill moose with it. He boiled with rage at this exhibition of their power, and suddenly took up the quarrel of the slain bull. But by no means did he lay aside his craft. Noiselessly he moved, a vast and furtive shadow, down through the thickets to a point where the underbrush nearly touched the water. This brought him within a few yards of the canoe, wherein the hunters had left their rifles. Here he paused a few moments, pondering. But as he pondered, redder and redder grew his eyes; and suddenly, with a mad roar, he burst from cover and charged.

Had the two men not been expert woodsmen, one or the other would have been caught and smashed to pulp. But their senses were on the watch. Cut off as they were from the canoe and from their weapons, their only hope was a tree. Before the king was fairly out into view, they had understood the whole situation, sprung to their feet, and sped off like hares. Just within the nearest fringe of bushes grew a low-hanging beech-tree; and into this they swung themselves, just as the king came raging beneath. As it was, one of them was nearly caught when he imagined himself quite safe. The king reared his mighty bulk against the trunk and with his keen-spiked antlers reached upward fiercely after the fugitives, the nearest of whom was saved only by a friendly branch which intervened.

For nearly an hour the king stamped and stormed beneath the branches, while the trapped hunters alternately cursed his temper and wondered at his stature. Then, with a swift change of purpose, he wheeled and charged on the canoe. In two minutes the graceful craft was reduced to raw material,— while the hunters in the tree-top, sputtering furiously, vowed vengeance. All the kit, the tins, the blankets, the boxes, were battered shapeless, and the rifles thumped well down into the wet sand. In the midst of the cataclysm, one of the rifles somehow went off. The noise and the flash astonished the king, but only added to his rage and made him more thorough in his work of destruction. When there was nothing left that seemed worth trampling upon, he returned to the tree, — on which he had kept eye all the time, — and there nursed his wrath all night. At the first of dawn, however, he came to the conclusion that the shivering things in the tree were not worth waiting for. He swung off, and sought his favourite pasturage, a mile or two away; and the men, after making sure of his departure, climbed down. They nervously cut some steaks from the bull which they had killed, and hurried away, crestfallen, on the long tramp back to the settlements.

This incident, however, did not have the effect which it might have been expected to have. It did not make the king despise men. On the contrary, he now knew them to be dangerous, and he also knew that their chief power lay in the long dark tubes which spit fire and made fierce sounds. It was enough for him that he had once worsted them. Ever afterward he gave them wide berth. And the tradition of him would have come at last to be doubted in the settlements, but for the vast, shed antlers occasionally found lying on the diminished snows of March.

But all the time, while the king waxed huge and wise, and overthrew his enemies, and begot great offspring that, for many years after he was dead, were to make the Mamozekel famous, there was one

The King of the Mamozekel 333

grave incompleteness in his sovereignty. His old panic fear of bears still shamed and harassed him. The whiff of a harmless half-grown cub, engrossed in stuffing its greedy red mouth with blueberries, was enough to turn his blood to water and send him off to other feeding-grounds. He chose his ranges, indeed, first of all for their freedom from the dreaded taint, and only second for the excellence of their pasturage. This one unreasoning fear was the drop of gall which went far toward embittering all the days of his singularly favoured life. It was as if the wood-gods, after endowing him so far beyond his fellows, had repented of their lavishness, and capriciously poisoned their gifts.

One autumn night, just at the beginning of the calling season, this weakness of his betrayed the king to the deepest humiliation which had ever befallen him. He was then nearly seven years old; and because his voice was known to every bull in the Tobique country, there was never answer made when his great challenge went stridently resounding over the moonlit wastes. But on this particular night, when he had roared perhaps for his own amusement, or for the edification of his mate who browsed near by, rather than with any expectation of response, to his astonishment there came an answering defiance from the other side of the open. A big, wandering bull, who had strayed up from the Grand River region, had never heard of the king, and was more than ready to put his valour to test. The king rushed to meet him. Now it chanced that between the approaching giants was an old ash-tree growing out of a thicket. In this thicket a bear had been grubbing for roots. When he heard the king's first roar, he started to steal away from the perilous proximity; but the second bull's answer, from the direction in which he had hoped to retreat, stopped him. In much perturbation he climbed the ash-tree to a safe distance, and curled himself into a black, furry ball, in a fork of the branches.

The night was still, and no scents wafting to sensitive nostrils. With short roars, and much thrashing of the underbrush, the two bulls drew near. When the king was just about abreast of the bear's hiding-place, his arrogance broke into fury, and he charged upon the audacious stranger. Just as he did so, and just as his foe sprang to meet him, a wilful night-wind puffed lightly through the branches. It was a very small, irresponsible wind; but it carried sharply to the king's nostrils the strong, fresh taint of bear.

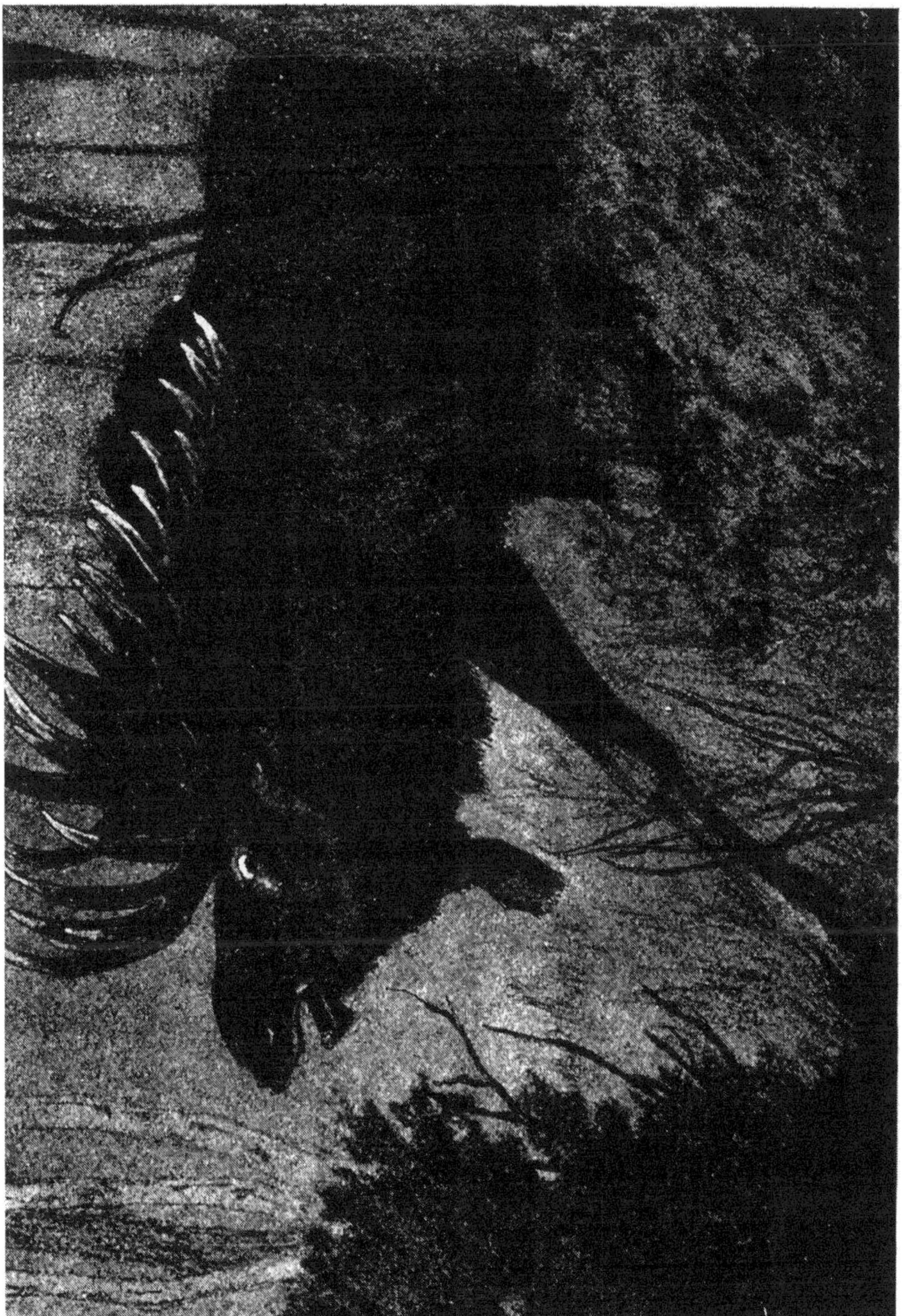

The smell was so strong, it seemed to the king as if the bear must be fairly on his haunches. It was like an icy cataract flung upon him. He shrank, trembled, — and the old wounds twinged and cringed. The next moment, to the triumphant amazement of his antagonist, he had wheeled aside to avoid the charge, and was off through the underbrush in ignominious flight. The newcomer, who, for all his stout-heartedness, had viewed with concern the giant bulk of his foe, stopped short in his tracks and stared in bewilderment. So easy a victory as this was beyond his dreams, — even beyond his desires. However, a bull moose can be a philosopher on occasion, and this one was not going to quarrel with good luck. In high elation he strode on up the meadow, and set himself, not unsuccessfully, to wooing the deserted and disgusted cow.

His triumph, however, was short-lived. About moon-rise of the following night the king came back. He was no longer thinking of bears, and his heart was full of wrath. His vast challenge came down from the near-by hills, making the night resound with its short, explosive thunders. His approach was accompanied by the thrashing of giant antlers on the trees, and by a crashing as if the undergrowths were being trodden by a locomotive. There was grim omen in the sounds; and the cow, waving her great ears back and forward thoughtfully, eyed the Grand River bull with shrewd interest. The stranger showed himself game, no whit daunted by threatenings and thunder. He answered with brave roarings, and manifested every resolution to maintain his conquest. But sturdy and valorous though he was, all his prowess went for little when the king fell upon him, thrice terrible from the memory of his humiliation. There was no such thing as withstanding that awful charge. Before it the usurper was borne back, borne down, overwhelmed, as if he had been no more than a yearling calf. He had no chance to recover. He was trampled and ripped and thrust onward, a helpless sprawl of unstrung legs and outstretched, piteous neck. It was luck alone, — or some unwonted kindness of the wood-spirits, — that saved his life from being trodden and beaten out in that hour of terror. It was close to the river-bank that he had made his stand; and presently, to his great good fortune, he was thrust over the brink. He fell into the water with a huge splash. When he struggled to his feet, and moved off, staggering, down the shallow edges of the stream, the king looked over and disdained to follow up the vengeance.

Fully as he had vindicated himself, the king was never secure against such a humiliation so long as he rested thrall to his one fear. The threat of the bear hung over him, a mystery of terror which he could not bring himself to face. But at last, and in the season of his weakness, when he had shed his antlers, there came a day when he was forced to face it. Then his kingliness was put to the supreme trial.

He was now at the age of nine years, in the splendour of his prime. He stood over seven feet high at the shoulders, and weighed perhaps thirteen hundred pounds. His last antlers, those which he had shed two months before, had shown a gigantic spread of nearly six feet.

It was late April. Much honeycombed snow and ice still lingered in the deeper hollows. After a high fashion of his own, seldom followed among the moose of the Tobique region, the king had rejoined his mate when she emerged from her spring retreat with a calf at her flank. He was too lordly in spirit to feel cast down or discrowned when his head was shorn of its great ornament; and he never felt the spring moroseness which drives most bull moose into seclusion. He always liked to keep his little herd together, was tolerant to the yearlings, and even refrained from driving off the two-year-olds until their own aggressiveness made it necessary.

On this particular April day, the king was bestriding a tall poplar sapling, which he had borne down that he might browse upon its tender, sap-swollen tips. By the water's edge the cow and the yearling were foraging on the young willow shoots. The calf, a big-framed, enterprising youngster two weeks old, almost as fine a specimen of young moosehood as the king had been at his age, was poking about curiously to gather knowledge of the wilderness world. He approached a big gray-white boulder, whose base was shrouded in spruce scrub, and sniffed apprehensively at a curious, pungent taint that came stealing out upon the air.

He knew by intuition that there was peril in that strange scent; but his interest overweighed his caution, and he drew close to the spruce scrub. Close, and yet closer; and his movement was so unusual that it attracted the attention of the king, who stopped browsing to watch him intently. A vague, only half-realised memory of that far-off day when he himself, a lank calf of the season, went sniffing curiously at a thicket, stirred in his brain; and the stiff hair along his neck and shoulder began to bristle. He released the poplar sapling, and turned all his attention to the behaviour of the calf.

The calf was very close to the green edges of the spruce scrub, when he caught sight of a great dark form within, which had revealed itself by a faint movement. More curious than ever, but now distinctly alarmed, he shrank back, turning at the same time, as if to investigate from another and more open side of the scrub.

The next instant a black bulk lunged forth with incredible swiftness from the green, and a great paw swung itself with a circular, sweeping motion, upon the retreating calf. In the wilderness world, as in the world of men, history has a trick of repeating itself; and this time, as on that day nine years before, the bear was just too late. The blow did not reach its object till most of its force was spent. It drew blood, and knocked the calf sprawling, but did no serious damage. With a bleat of pain and terror, the little animal jumped to its feet and ran away.

The bear would have easily caught him before he could recover himself; but another and very different voice had answered the bleat of the calf. At the king's roar of fury the bear changed his plans and slunk back into hiding. In a moment the king came thundering up to the edge of the spruces. There, planting his fore-feet suddenly till they ploughed the ground, he stopped himself with a mighty effort. The smell of the bear had smitten him in the face.

The moment was a crucial one. The pause was full of fate. Turning his head in indecision, he caught a cry of pain from the calf as it ran to its mother; and he saw the blood streaming down its flank. Then the kingliness of his heart arose victorious. With a roar, he breasted trampling into the spruce scrub, heedless at last of the dreaded scent.

The bear, meanwhile, had been seeking escape. He had just emerged on the other side of the spruces, and was slipping off to find a secure tree. As the king thundered down upon him, he wheeled with a savage growl, half squatted back, and struck out sturdily with that redoubtable paw. But at the same instant the king's edged hoofs came down upon him with the impact of a battering ram. They smashed in his ribs. They tore open his side. They hurled him over so that his belly was exposed. He was at a hopeless disadvantage. He had not an instant for recovery. Those avenging hoofs, with

"IT WAS FEAR ITSELF THAT HE WAS WIPING OUT."

the power of a pile-driver behind them, smote like lightning. The bear struck savagely, twice, thrice; and his claws tore their way through hide and muscle till the king's blood gushed scarlet over his prostrate foe's dark fur. Then, the growls and the claw-strokes ceased; and the furry shape lay still, outstretched, unresisting.

For a moment or two the king drew off, and eyed the carcass. Then the remembrance of all his past terror and shame surged hotly through him. He pounced again upon the body, and pounded it, and trampled it, and ground it down, till the hideous mass bore no longer a resemblance to any thing that ever carried the breath of life. It was not his enemy only, not only the assailant of the helpless calf, that he was thus completely blotting from existence, but it was fear itself that he was wiping out.

At last, grown suddenly tired of rage, and somewhat faint from the red draining of his veins, the king turned away and sought his frightened herd. They gathered about him, trembling with excitement, — the light-coated cow, the dark yearling, the lank, terrified calf. They stretched thin noses toward him, questioning, wondering, troubled at his hot, streaming wounds. But the king held his head high, heeding neither the wounds nor the herd. He cast one long, proud look up the valley of the Mamozekel, his immediate, peculiar domain. Then he looked southward over the lonely Serpentine, northward across the dark-wooded Nictau, and westward down the flood of the full, united stream. He felt himself supreme now beyond challenge over all the wild lands of Tobique.

For a long time the group stood so, breathing at last quietly, still with that stillness which the furtive kindreds know. There was no sound save the soft, ear-filling roar of the three rivers, swollen with freshet, rushing gladly to their confluence. The sound was as a background to the cool, damp silence of the April wilderness. Some belated snow in a shaded hollow close at hand shrank and settled, with a hushed, evasive whisper. Then the earliest white-throat, from the top of a fir-tree, fluted across the pregnant spring solitudes the six clear notes of his musical and melancholy call.

IN PANOPLY OF SPEARS

In Panoply of Spears

THERE was a pleasant humming all about the bee-tree, where it stood solitary on the little knoll upon the sunward slope of the forest. It was an ancient maple, one side long since blasted by lightning, and now decayed to the heart; while the other side yet put forth a green bravery of branch and leaf. High up under a dead limb was a hole, thronged about with diligent bees who came and went in long diverging streams against the sun-steeped blue. A mile below, around the little, straggling backwoods settlement, the buckwheat was in bloom; and the bees counted the longest day too short for the gathering of its brown and fragrant sweets.

In fine contrast to their bustle and their haste was a moveless dark brown figure clinging to a leafy branch on the other and living side of the tree. From a distance it might easily have been taken for a big bird's-nest. Far out on the limb it sat, huddled into a bristling ball. Its nose, its whole head indeed, were hidden between its fore paws, which childishly but tenaciously clutched at a little upright branch. In this position, seemingly so precarious, but really, for the porcupine, the safest and most comfortable that could be imagined, it dozed away the idle summer hours.

From the thick woods at the foot of the knoll emerged a large black bear, who lifted his nose and eyed shrewdly the humming streams of workers converging at the hole in the bee-tree. For some time the bear stood contemplative, till an eager light grew in his small, cunning, half-humourous eyes. His long red tongue came out and licked his lips, as he thought of the summer's sweetness now stored in the hollow tree. He knew all about that prosperous bee colony. He remembered when, two years before, the runaway swarm from the settlement had taken possession of the hole in the old maple. That same autumn he had tried to rifle the treasure-house, but had found the wood about the entrance still too sound and strong for even such powerfully rending claws as his. He had gone away surly with disappointment, to scratch a few angry bees out of his fur, and wait for the natural processes of decay to weaken the walls of the citadel.

On this particular day he decided to try again.

He had no expectation that he would succeed; but the thought of the honey grew irresistible to him as he dwelt upon it. He lumbered lazily up the knoll, reared his dark bulk against the trunk, and started to climb to the attack.

But the little workers in the high-set hive found an unexpected protector in this hour of their need. The dozing porcupine woke up, and took it into his head that he wanted to go somewhere else. Perhaps in his dreams a vision had come to him of the lonely little oat-field in the clearing, where the young grain was plumping out and already full of milky sweetness. As a rule he preferred to travel and feed by night. But the porcupine is the last amid the wild kindreds to let convention interfere with impulse, and he does what seems good to the whim of the moment. His present whim was to descend the bee-tree and journey over to the clearing.

The bear had climbed but seven or eight feet, when he heard the scraping of claws on the bark above. He heard also the light clattering noise, unlike any other sound in the wilderness. He knew it at once as the sound of the loose-hung, hollow quills in a porcupine's active tail; and looking up angrily, he saw the porcupine curl himself downward from a crotch and begin descending the trunk to meet him.

The bear weighed perhaps four hundred or five hundred pounds. The porcupine weighed perhaps twenty-five pounds. Nevertheless, the bear stopped; and the porcupine came on. When he saw the bear, he gnashed his teeth irritably, and his quills, his wonderful panoply of finely barbed spears, erected themselves all over his body till his usual bulk seemed doubled. At the same time his colour changed. It was almost as if he had grown suddenly pale with indignation; for when the long quills stood up from among his blackish-brown fur they showed themselves all white save for their dark keen points. Small as he was in comparison with his gigantic opponent, he looked, nevertheless, curiously formidable. He grunted and grumbled querulously, and came on with confidence, obstinately proclaiming that no mere bear should for a moment divert him from his purpose.

Whether by instinct, experience, or observation, the bear knew something about porcupines. What would honey be to him, with two or three of those slender and biting spear-points embedded in his nose? As he thought of it, he backed away with increasing alacrity. He checked a rash impulse

"THE BEAR EYED HIM FOR SOME MOMENTS"

to dash the arrogant little hinderer from the tree and annihilate him with one stroke of his mighty paw, — but the mighty paw cringed, winced, and drew back impotent, as its sensitive nerves considered how it would feel to be stuck full, like a pincushion, with inexorably penetrating points. At last, thoroughly outfaced, the bear descended to the ground, and stood aside respectfully for the porcupine to pass.

The porcupine, however, on reaching the foot of the trunk, discovered an uncertainty in his mind. His whim wavered. He stopped, scratched his ears thoughtfully first with one fore paw and then with the other, and tried his long, chisel-like front teeth, those matchless gnawing machines, on a projecting edge of bark. The bear eyed him for some moments, then lumbered off into the woods indifferently, convinced that the bee-tree would be just as interesting on some other day. But before that other day came around, the bear encountered Fate, lying in wait for him, grim and implacable, beneath a trapper's deadfall in the heart of the tamarack swamp. And the humming tribes in the bee-tree were left to possess their honeyed commonwealth in peace.

Soon after the bear had left the knoll, the porcupine appeared to make up his mind as to what he wanted to do. With an air of fixed purpose he started down the knoll, heading for the oat-field and the clearing which lay some half-mile distant through the woods. As he moved on the ground, he was a somewhat clumsy and wholly grotesque figure. He walked with a deliberate and precise air, very slowly, and his legs worked as if the earth were to them an unfamiliar element. He was about two and a half feet long, short-legged, solid and sturdy looking, with a nose curiously squared off so that it should not get in the way of his gnawing. As he confronted you, his great chisel teeth, bared and conspicuous, appeared a most formidable weapon. Effective as they were, however, they were not a weapon which he was apt to call into use, save against inanimate and edible opponents; because he could not do so without exposing his weak points to attack, — his nose, his head, his soft, unprotected throat. His real weapon of offence was his short, thick tail, which was heavily armed with very powerful quills. With this he could strike slashing blows, such as would fill an enemy's face or paws with spines, and send him howling from the encounter. Clumsy and inert it looked, on ordinary occasions; but when need arose, its muscles had the lightning action of a strong steel spring.

In Panoply of Spears

As the porcupine made his resolute way through the woods, the manner of his going differed from that of all the other kindreds of the wild. He went not furtively. He had no particular objection to making a noise. He did not consider it necessary to stop every little while, stiffen himself to a monument of immobility, cast wary glances about the gloom, and sniff the air for the taint of enemies. He did not care who knew of his coming; and he did not greatly care who came. Behind his panoply of biting spears he felt himself secure, and in that security he moved as if he held in fee the whole green, shadowy, perilous woodland world.

A wood-mouse, sitting in the door of his burrow between the roots of an ancient fir-tree, went on washing his face with his dainty paws as the porcupine passed within three feet of him. Almost any other forest traveller would have sent the timid mouse darting to the depths of his retreat; but he knew that the slow-moving figure, however terrible to look at, had no concern for wood-mice. The porcupine had barely passed, however, when a weasel came in view. In a flash the mouse was gone, to lie hidden for an hour, with trembling heart, in the furthest darkness of his burrow.

Continuing his journey, the porcupine passed

under a fallen tree. Along the horizontal trunk lay a huge lynx, crouched flat, movelessly watching for rabbit, chipmunk, mink, or whatever quarry might come within his reach. He was hungry, as a lynx is apt to be. He licked his chaps, and his wide eyes paled with savage fire, as the porcupine dawdled by beneath the tree, within easy clutch of his claws. But his claws made no least motion of attack. He, too, like the bear, knew something about porcupines. In a few moments, however, when the porcupine had gone on some ten or twelve feet beyond his reach, his feelings overcame him so completely that he stood up and gave vent to an appalling scream of rage. All the other wild things within hearing trembled at the sound, and were still; and the porcupine, startled out of his equipoise, tucked his nose between his legs, and bristled into a ball of sharp defiance. The lynx eyed him venomously for some seconds, then dropped lightly from the perch, and stole off to hunt in other neighbourhoods, realising that his reckless outburst of bad temper had warned all the coverts for a quarter of a mile around. The porcupine, uncurling, grunted scornfully and resumed his journey.

Very still, and lonely and bright the clearing lay in the flooding afternoon sunshine. It lay along beside a deeply rutted, grass-grown backwoods road which had been long forgotten by the attentions of the road-master. It was enclosed from the forest in part by a dilapidated wall of loose stones, in part by an old snake fence, much patched with brush. The cabin which had once presided over its solitude had long fallen to ruin; but its fertile soil had saved it from being forgotten. A young farmer-lumberman from the settlement a couple of miles away held possession of it, and kept its boundaries more or less intact, and made it yield him each year a crop of oats, barley, or buckwheat.

Emerging from the woods, the porcupine crawled to the top of the stone wall and glanced about him casually. Then he descended into the cool, light-green depths of the growing oats. Here he was completely hidden, though his passage was indicated as he went by the swaying and commotion among the oat-tops.

The high plumes of the grain, of course, were far above the porcupine's reach; and for a healthy appetite like his it would have been tedious work indeed to pull down the stalks one by one. At this point, he displayed an ingenious resourcefulness with which he is seldom credited by observers of his kind. Because he is slow in movement, folk are apt to conclude that he is slow in wit; whereas the truth is that he has fine reserves of shrewdness to fall back on in emergency. Instead of pulling and treading down the oats at haphazard, he moved through the grain in a small circle, leaning heavily inward. When he had thus gone around the circle several times, the tops of the grain lay together in a convenient bunch. This succulent sheaf he dragged down, and devoured with relish.

When he had abundantly satisfied his craving for young oats, he crawled out upon the open sward by the fence, and carelessly sampled the bark of a seedling apple-tree. While he was thus engaged a big, yellow dog came trotting up the wood-road, poking his nose inquisitively into every bush and stump in the hope of finding a rabbit or chipmunk to chase. He belonged to the young farmer who owned the oat-field; and when, through the rails of the snake fence, he caught sight of the porcupine, he was filled with noisy wrath. Barking and yelping, — partly with excitement, and partly as a signal to his master who was trudging along the road far behind him, — he clambered over the fence, and bore down upon the trespasser.

The porcupine was not greatly disturbed by this loud onslaught, but he did not let confidence make

In Panoply of Spears 361

him careless. He calmly tucked his head under his breast, set his quills in battle array, and awaited the event with composure.

Had he discovered the porcupine in the free woods, the yellow dog would have let him severely alone. But in his master's oat-field, that was a different matter. Moreover, the knowledge that his master was coming added to his zeal and rashness; and he had long cherished the ambition to kill a porcupine. He sprang forward, open-jawed, — and stopped short when his fangs were just within an inch or two of those bristling and defiant points. Caution had come to his rescue just in time.

For perhaps half a minute he ran, whining and baffled, around the not-to-be daunted ball of spines. Then he sat down upon his haunches, lifted up his muzzle, and howled for his master to come and help him.

As his master failed to appear within three seconds, his impatience got the better of him, and he again began running around the porcupine, snapping fiercely, but never coming within two or three inches of the militant points. For a few moments these two or three inches proved to be a safe distance. Such a distance from the shoulders, back, and sides was all well enough. But suddenly, he was so misguided as to bring his teeth together within a couple of inches of the armed but quiescent tail. This was the instant for which the porcupine had been waiting. The tail flicked smartly. The big dog jumped, gave a succession of yelping cries, pawed wildly at his nose, then tucked his tail between his legs, scrambled over the fence, and fled away to his master. The porcupine unrolled himself, and crawled into an inviting hole in the old stone wall.

About ten minutes later a very angry man, armed with a fence-stake, appeared at the edge of the clearing with a cowed dog at his heels. He wanted to find the porcupine which had stuck those quills into his dog's nose. Mercifully merciless, he had held the howling dog in a grip of iron while he pulled out the quills with his teeth; and now he was after vengeance. Knowing a little, but not everything, about porcupines, he searched every tree in the immediate neighbourhood, judging that the porcupine, after such an encounter, would make all haste to his natural retreat. But he never looked in the hole in the wall; and the yellow dog, who had come to doubt the advisability of finding porcupines, refused firmly to assist in the search. In a little while, when his anger began to cool, he gave over the hunt in disgust, threw away the fence-stake, bit off a goodly chew from the fig of black tobacco which he produced from his hip-pocket, and strode away up the grassy wood-road.

For perhaps half an hour the porcupine dozed in the hole among the stones. Then he woke up, crawled out, and moved slowly along the top of the wall.

There was a sound of children's voices coming up the road; but the porcupine, save for a grumble of impatience, paid no attention. Presently the children came in sight, — a stocky little boy of nine or ten, and a lank girl of perhaps thirteen, making their way homeward from school by the short cut over the mountain. Both were barefooted and barelegged, deeply freckled, and with long, tow-coloured locks. The boy wore a shirt and short breeches of blue-gray homespun, the breeches held up precariously by one suspender. On his head was a tattered and battered straw; and in one hand he swung a little tin dinner-pail. The girl wore the like blue-gray homespun for a petticoat, with a waist of bright red calico, and carried a limp pink sunbonnet on her arm.

"Oh, see the porkypine!" cried the girl, as they came abreast of the stone wall.

"By gosh! Let's kill it!" exclaimed the stocky

little boy, starting forward eagerly, with a prompt efflorescence of primitive instincts. But his sister clutched him by the arm and anxiously restrained him.

"My lands, Jimmy, you musn't go near a porkypine like that!" she protested, more learned than her brother in the hoary myths of the settlements. "Don't you know he can fling them quills of his'n at you, an' they'll go right through an' come out the other side?"

"By gosh!" gasped the boy, eyeing the unconcerned animal with apprehension, and edging off to the furthermost ditch. Hand in hand, their eyes wide with excitement, the two children passed beyond the stone wall. Then, as he perceived that the porcupine had not seemed to notice them, the boy's hunting instinct revived. He stopped, set down the tin dinner-pail, and picked up a stone.

"No, you don't, Jimmy!" intervened the girl, with mixed emotions of kindliness and caution, as she grabbed his wrist and dragged him along.

"Why, Sis?" protested the boy, hanging back, and looking over his shoulder longingly. "Jest let me fling a stone at him!"

"No!" said his sister, with decision. "He ain't a-hurtin' us, an' he's mindin' his own business. An'

I reckon maybe he can fling quills as fur as you can fling stones!"

Convinced by this latter argument, the boy gave up his design, and suffered his wise sister to lead him away from so perilous a neighbourhood. The two little figures vanished amid the green glooms beyond the clearing, and the porcupine was left untroubled in his sovereignty.

II.

That autumn, late one moonlight night, the porcupine was down by a little forest lake feasting on lily pads. He occupied a post of great advantage, a long, narrow ledge of rock jutting out into the midst of the lilies, and rising but an inch or two above the water. Presently, to his great indignation, he heard a dry rustling of quills behind him, and saw another porcupine crawl out upon his rock. He faced about, bristling angrily and gnashing his teeth, and advanced to repel the intruder.

The intruder hesitated, then came on again with confidence, but making no hostile demonstrations whatever. When the two met, the expected conflict was by some sudden agreement omitted. They touched blunt noses, squeaked and grunted together for awhile till a perfect understanding was established; then crawled ashore and left the lily pads to rest, broad, shiny, and unruffled in the moonlight, little platters of silver on the dark glass of the lake.

The newcomer was a female; and with such brief wooing the big porcupine had taken her for his mate. Now he led her off to show her the unequalled den which he had lately discovered. The den was high in the side of a heap of rocks, dry in all weathers, and so overhung by a half-uprooted tree as to be very well concealed from passers and prowlers. Its entrance was long and narrow, deterrent to rash investigators. In fact, just after the porcupine had moved in, a red fox had discovered the doorway and judged it exactly to his liking; but on finding that the occupant was a porcupine, he had hastily decided to seek accommodation elsewhere. In this snug house the two porcupines settled contentedly for the winter.

The winter passed somewhat uneventfully for them, though for the rest of the wood-folk it was a season of unwonted hardship. The cold was more intense and more implacable than had been known about the settlements for years. Most of the wild creatures, save those who could sleep the bitter months away and abide the coming of spring, found themselves face to face with famine. But the porcupines feared neither famine nor cold. The brown fur beneath their quills was thick and warm, and hunger was impossible to them with all the trees of the forest for their pasturage. Sometimes, when the cold made them sluggish, they would stay all day and all night in a single balsam-fir or hemlock, stripping one branch after another of leaf and twig, indifferent to the monotony of their diet. At other times, however, they were as active and enterprising as if all the heats of summer were loosing their sinews. On account of the starvation-madness that was everywhere ranging the coverts, they were more than once attacked as they crawled lazily over the snow; but on each occasion the enemy, whether lynx or fox, fisher or mink, withdrew discomfited, with something besides hunger in his hide to think about.

Once, in midwinter, they found a prize which added exquisite variety to their bill of fare. Having wandered down to the outskirts of the settlements, they discovered, cast aside among the bushes, an empty firkin which had lately contained salt pork. The wood, saturated with brine, was delicious to the porcupines. Greedily they gnawed at it, returning night after night to the novel banquet, till the last sliver of the flavoured wood was gone. Then, after lingering a day or two longer in the neighbourhood, expecting another miracle, they returned to their solitudes and their hemlock.

When winter was drawing near its close, but spring had not yet sent the wilderness word of her coming, the porcupines got her message in their blood. They proclaimed it abroad in the early twilight from the tops of the high hemlocks, in queer, half-rhythmical choruses of happy grunts and squeaks. The sound was far from melodious, but it pleased every one of the wild kindred to whose ears it came; for they knew that when the porcupines got trying to sing, then the spring thaws were hurrying up from the south.

At last the long desired one came; and every little rill ran a brawling brook in the fulness of its joy. And the ash-buds swelled rich purple; and the maples crimsoned with their misty blooms; and the skunk cabbage began to thrust up bold knobs of emerald, startling in their brightness, through the black and naked leaf-mould of the swamp. And just at this time, when all the wild kindred, from the wood-mouse to the moose, felt sure that life was good, a porcupine baby was born in the snug den among the rocks.

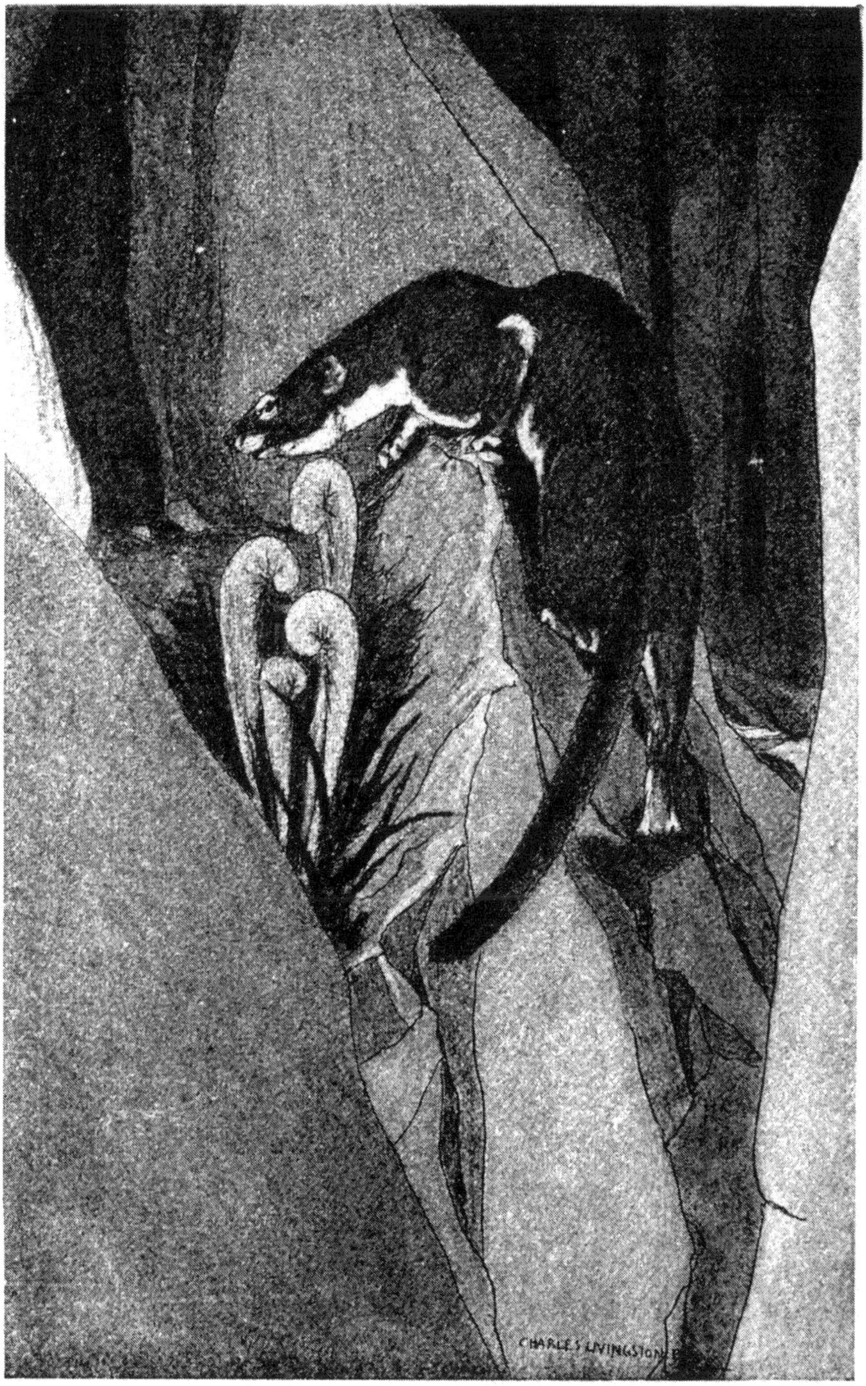
CHARLES LIVINGSTON

In Panoply of Spears

It was an astonishingly big baby,— the biggest, in proportion to the size of its parents, of all the babies of the wild. In fact it was almost as big as an average bear cub. It was covered with long, dark brown, silky fur, under which the future panoply of spear-points was already beginning to make way through the tender skin. Its mother was very properly proud, and assiduous in her devotion. And the big father, though seemingly quite indifferent, kept his place contentedly in the den instead of going off sourly by himself to another lair as the porcupine male is apt to do on the arrival of the young.

One evening about dusk, when the young porcupine was but three days old, a weasel glided noiselessly up to the door of the den, and sniffed. His eyes, set close together and far down toward his malignant, pointed nose, were glowing red with the lust of the kill. Fierce and fearless as he was, he knew well enough that a porcupine was something for him to let alone. But this, surely, was his chance to feed fat an ancient grudge; for he hated everything that he could not hope to kill. He had seen the mother porcupine feeding comfortably in the top of a near-by poplar. And now he made assurance doubly sure by sniffing at her trail, which came out from the den and did not return. As for the big male porcupine, the prowler took it for granted that he had followed the usage of his kind, and gone off about other business. Like a snake, he slipped in, and found the furry baby all alone. There was a strong, squeaking cry, a moment's struggle; and then the weasel drank eagerly at the blood of his easy prey. The blood, and the fierce joy of the kill, were all he wanted, for his hunting was only just begun.

The assassin stayed but a minute with his victim, then turned swiftly to the door of the den. But the door was blocked. It was filled by an ominous, bristling bulk, which advanced upon him slowly, inexorably, making a sharp, clashing sound with its long teeth. The big porcupine had come home. And his eyes blazed more fiercely red than those of the weasel.

The weasel, fairly caught, felt that doom was upon him. He backed away, over the body of his victim, to the furthest depth of the den. But, though a ruthless murderer, the most cruel of all the wild kindred, he was no coward. He would evade the slow avenger if he could; but if not, he would fight to the last gasp.

Against this foe the porcupine scorned his customary tactics, and depended upon his terrible, cutting teeth. At the same time he knew that the weasel was desperate and deadly. Therefore he held his head low, shielding his tender throat. When he reached the wider part of the den, he suddenly swung sidewise, thus keeping the exit still blocked.

Seeing now that there was no escape, the weasel gathered his forces for one last fight. Like lightning he sprang, and struck; and being, for speed, quite matchless among the wild folk, he secured a deadly hold on the porcupine's jaw. The porcupine squeaked furiously and tried to shake his adversary off. With a sweep of his powerful neck, he threw the weasel to one side, and then into the air over his head.

The next instant the weasel came down, sprawling widely, full upon the stiffly erected spears of the porcupine's back. They pierced deep into his tender belly. With a shrill cry he relaxed his hold on the avenger's jaw, shrank together in anguish, fell to the ground, and darted to the exit. As he passed he got a heavy slap from the porcupine's tail, which filled his face and neck with piercing barbs. Then he escaped from the den and fled away toward his own lair, carrying his death with him. Before he had gone a hundred yards one of the quills in his belly reached a vital part. He faltered, fell, stretched his legs out weakly, and died. Then a red squirrel, who had been watching him in a quiver of fear and hate, shot from his hiding-place, ran wildly up and down his tree, and made the woods ring with his sharp, barking chatter of triumph over the death of the universal enemy.

In the midst of the squirrel's shrill rejoicings the porcupine emerged from his den. He seemed to hesitate, which is not the way of a porcupine. He looked at his mate, still foraging in the top of her poplar, happily unaware for the present of how her little world had changed. He seemed to realise that the time of partings had come, the time when he must resume his solitude. He turned and looked at his den, — he would never find another like it! Then he crawled off through the cool, wet woods, where the silence seemed to throb sweetly with the stir and fulness of the sap. And in a hollow log, not far from the bee-tree on the knoll, he found himself a new home, small and solitary.

THE END.

Lightning Source UK Ltd.
Milton Keynes UK
UKHW021829201122
412546UK00004B/12